GAME IN THE KITCHEN

COOKERY FOR NIMRODS,

GAME IN THE

ILLUSTRATIONS BY PAUL GIAMBARBA

BARRE PUBLISHERS

ANGLERS AND THEIR FRIENDS

KITCHEN

BY BARBARA FLOOD
EDITED BY WILLAN C. ROUX

WITH A PREFACE BY DANA S. LAMB

BARRE, MASSACHUSETTS

STANDARD BOOK NUMBER 8271-7241-9
LIBRARY OF CONGRESS CARD NUMBER 68-29798
COPYRIGHT © 1968 BY BARBARA FLOOD AND WILLAN C. ROUX
BARRE PUBLISHERS, BARRE, MASSACHUSETTS
DESIGNED BY PAUL GIAMBARBA

To my husband H. Carson Flood
without whose encouragement this book
might never have been written.

To Izaak Hunter, editor of the Rod & Gun Column
    in the Montreal Gazette
—Yves Louis Ploneis, Chef of the 21 Club, N.Y.C.
—Elisabeth Princess Altenburg of Austria
— Mary von Motzeck, South Carolina
— T. T. Saunders, Kitchen Manager of Magdalen
    College, Cambridge, England
— Raymond Ferry, Chef de Cuisine of the Mount Royal
    Club, Montreal, Canada
— Lydia Kakko
—Jim Wright
—Harvey H. Smith
— Malise Skillings
    and finally to my editor Bill Roux.

PREFACE

So pleasant, over the years, have been those sporting journeys which have taken me to Montreal and Maine that I can perhaps justly be accused of a predisposition in favor of the works of any resident of those areas whose sporting interests more or less coincide with mine. Nevertheless, I feel that I can say without challenge that Barbara Flood — with an able assist from Willan Roux—has compiled in *Game in The Kitchen* instructions so complete as to the handling of fish and game from the moment of its capture to its appearance on the table that the sportsman and his guests may be guaranteed at home full enjoyment of the fruits of a straight shot on the mountainside or moor or of a careful cast with the proper fly on a trout or salmon stream.

Between the extremes of Farley Mowat's, Souris à la Crême and Sam Weller's "weal pie" the authors have covered the sportsman's gastronomic field as comprehensively as a Lord Macaulay covering England's eighteenth century. Nor has this been done without a seasoning of penache and humor.

Let the reader but dwell for a few delicious moments on Barbara Flood's account of the dinner of the Grand Romaine

Salmon Club. Let him note her advice to "take (his) best girl frog hunting some warm moonlit summer night. Catch some frogs (she says) but don't be such an eager beaver that you devote all your attention to the frogs."

With this excellent book handy in the kitchen (and I would suggest another copy in the library), fortunate indeed will be those guests who may be favored by a dinner invitation.

Dana S. Lamb

AUTHOR'S FOREWORD

Willan C. Roux, the author of two cookbooks, *What's Cooking Down in Maine* and *Fried Coffee and Jellied Bourbon* as well as a number of short stories, is the editor of this book. He has added immeasurably to the successful completion of *Game In The Kitchen* and I am more than grateful for his generous help. It was a great pleasure working with him and I extend my sincerest thanks.

Barbara Flood
Montreal, P. Q., Canada

CONTENTS

MEET BARBARA FLOOD

Barbara Flood is a unique person: a charming lady whose cosmopolitan background and social graces belie her great aptitude in the woods, the fields, and on the water. And she is as proficient a cook as she is an expert huntress and fisherwoman. I am proud to introduce her to you and to recommend this, her book.

Living in Canada, as they do, the Floods have the happiest of hunting and fishing grounds virtually in their back yard. The variety of edible game — animal, fowl and fish — that is found there is more than enough to provide sport and food the year round. But Canada has been only one of the many areas they have hunted and fished, having trekked far and wide in other parts of North America, several European countries and all of the British Isles. Even now, as I write this, they are somewhere in Canada where the fish are jumping and their rods are at the ready. I guarantee there will be trout or bass or salmon for dinner. And Barbara will cook it as skillfully as either she or her husband hooked it.

The instructions and recipes Barbara has put together in the following pages are top drawer, practical and easy to follow. They'll guide you safely and surely to your own gastronomic masterpieces. I know. I've used some of them.

When Barbara Flood asked me to join hands, so to speak, in putting this book into final form, I was happy to do it.

This, then, is Barbara's book—and a worthy one. What she has to say about game—bagging, preserving, preparing and cooking it—is authoritative and interestingly presented. My part in it has been a little organizing here, a bit of rewriting and editing there and a few cooking suggestions and recipes where they seemed appropriate.

Thus, if someone wants to give you game, by all means accept it and let Barbara Flood's expertise direct you in its care and cooking. Or, if you bag, catch or buy it yourself, you'll certainly profit by using her recipes. Good hunting—and good eating. They go together.

Willan C. Roux
Orr's Island, Maine

BARBARA FLOOD SPEAKING

Craig Claiborne, Food Editor of the New York Times, discovered recently in his travels around the country in search of regional recipes that "this is a nation with a deep-rooted interest in game and the preparation thereof. Duck, venison, rabbit, squirrel or whatever, all can be enjoyed in season and out since their meat freezes well."

The same is true of Canada and, of course, Europe and the British Isles. For years I have been a game addict, enjoying its preparation no less than its bagging. And this culinary collection is a result.

While I trust that sportsmen will find GAME IN THE KITCHEN of more than passing interest, I have written it primarily for their wives and their often perplexed friends. It is both a guide book and a cook book, a recording of my experience in the what-to-do and how-to-do of game preservation, preparation, cooking and serving.

Of paramount importance to eventual enjoyment at table are the proper handling and loving care of freshly bagged game, be it animal, fowl or fish. "What do I do with the ducks? . . . Are the fish cleaned? . . . Must I scale them? . . . Is the venison ready to cook? . . . Shall I pluck the pheasant? . . . How? . . . Will bear meat keep for any length of time?" These are only a few of the questions that will come to mind. Hopefully, this book will be of practical assistance in solving these and other dilemmas that can and do present themselves when well intentioned, proud hunters and fishermen arrive, bearing gifts from the wild.

Hunting and fishing with my dedicated husband, at first not exactly pleasurable, have developed, over the years, into challenging, rewarding pastimes. My husband has long since admitted me as an equal in the fields and woods and on lakes and streams. He is most appreciative that my legs can walk nearly as fast as his, that I can handle a gun rather well, manage the dogs, cast a line with reasonable skill and contrive, with pots and pans, in camp and at home, dishes that tickle his palate and reach his big heart through his approving stomach. He has flattered me with a true gourmet's accolade: an imaginary *cordon bleu*. Of course, he's prejudiced but, woman-like, I love it!

Game cooking in the Province of Quebec has always been considered excellent. While the French and the English have provided a distinguished game cuisine, the North Americans do not like game as *haut goût* (overly hung). Because game has its own distinct and often delicate flavor, we do not go along with the Europeans' preference for "high taint."

We do, however, go along with much of their cooking. As Irving Cobb, the American humorist, said "when the supreme cook of the universe arrives, he will be French, but will have served apprenticeship in Denmark, Russia, Austria and Italy." We have borrowed from them all, selectively and with sophistication. And our cooking, forthright and honest, shows it: it is international, incorporating much that

Europe offers, but plentifully seasoned with our own ideas and cooking practices.

Many of the recipes herein are my own developments, some original, others refinements, and — I think — improvements on those acquired from various sources. A number are pet dishes of well known personages and distinguished chefs. And a few are simple, campers' specials. I have included ways of using leftovers and of making chowders, soups, soufflés, salads and sauces. You will find, perhaps to your amazement, Braised Seal Flippers, Hot Crow's Nest, Ground Hog, Porcupine, Wild Boar, Corned Moose and Prairie Chicken.

And when there is no game in your larder you will discover that, in most of the recipes, you can substitute domestic animals and fowl and commercial types of fish with almost equal gustatory appeal.

May the sportsman's horn of plenty be yours to share, often and happily!

Barbara Flood
Montreal, Canada

THE GRAND ROMAINE SALMON
CLUB DINNER

On January 17, 1964, my husband sat down at table with members of the Grande Romaine Salmon Club at the Mount Royal Club in Montreal and enjoyed a feast of truly Lucullan proportions. It was a game dinner prepared and served in a manner that befitted the occasion and the surroundings. There were six courses, each accented by a superb, compatible wine. Appropriately, when the Haggis was brought in to the skirl of bagpipes, it was accompanied by a fine Scotch whisky - neat!

It was, according to Carson, a never-to-be-forgotten dinner which I just had to include in this book for you to admire — and envy. I have given the English translations of the French and Indian which were uninterpreted on the original menu. And you will note page numbers under each course indicating where the recipes and cooking techniques are to be found herein. (I'm sharing the wealth.) The chances are you will not attempt the complete dinner — all the game may not be available to you at one time. But, given a particular animal, fowl or fish, you will be able to enjoy these culinary masterpieces one by one.

THE MENU

Cocktails	Canapés Salar Fumé (Smoked Salmon, see page 154)
Harvey's Shooting Sherry	Amishk Oshui Muskemi (Clear Beaver Tail Soup, see page 175)
Chateau Pontet Canet 1959	Atsuk Flippers Giassonière (Braised Seal Flippers, see page 166)
	Purée Racine Le sorbet au Champagne
Chateau Haut Brion 1956	Poitrine de Perdrix avec Plomb (Breast of Partridge with "lead," see page 115) Riz Sauvage (Wild Rice)
Buchanan's DeLuxe Scotch Whisky	Haggis avec Cornemuses (A Scottish dish. "Avec Cornemuses" means with bagpipes . . . and yes, they were there)
Bollinger 1955	Pamplemousse Romanoff (Grapefruit cut out, replaced and topped with ginger and honey and served hot.)
Cognac Rémy Baccarat	Noix Petits Fours Menthes Demi Tasse

WHEN GAME COMES INTO
THE KITCHEN

There's nothing the least bit mysterious or complicated about game cookery — animal, fowl or fish. If you think of it as food and give to its preparation the care and imagination to bring out the best in it, you will discover, and delight in, its very special flavors and textures. There are choice cuts as well as lesser cuts just as there are in beef, lamb, pork or veal. Because it has more protein and less fat than domesticated animals, game is more easily digested and is thus often recommended for sick diets.

The meat of game birds is drier than that of domestic fowl but is generally as tender and succulent when properly processed and cooked. Fish is fish whether caught on a rod or brought in by commercial fishermen. Each variety has its own individuality: the flesh runs from dark and oily to pink and very white and firm. Methods of cooking should be determined by character and size.

The various kinds and cuts of game can be treated like domestic meats, fowl or fish once they are ready to be prepared for the table. The method of cooking — frying, sautéing, broiling, baking, roasting, boiling — is largely determined by what you have on hand: chops, steaks, roasts, stews, large or small birds and kinds and sizes of fish. All of the recipes herein give you adequate cues.

On practically all four-legged animals the fore quarters are much less tender than the saddle, loins and hind quarters. Many people, having eaten only cuts from the fore quarters, have decried the qualities of venison, moose, bear or other animals. Had they eaten the better cuts they would have been favorably impressed with the tenderness, texture and flavor of the meat. This is not to say that the lesser cuts cannot be incorporated into appetizing dishes. The way you cook them — and there are many suggestions on the following pages — establishes their worthiness.

Incidentally, if, by some remote chance, you come by a wild boar, you will find that the right hind leg is more tender than the left. That's because the boar rests on his right side and scratches himself with his left hind leg. The same is true, to an extent, of domestic hogs. The exercise toughens the meat!

There are two suggestions I want to insert right here. They are ways of assuring tender, juicy roasts or birds. Using parchment (*papillote*) or aluminum foil to enclose the meat is a simple and effective way to achieve moistness and even roasting. (Actually, a paper bag will serve the same purpose.) Generally speaking the covering should be removed after most of the cooking time has elapsed to allow the roast to brown. This is particularly important for pheasant and other feathered game or domestic fowl.

Accent or monosodium glutinate are splendid tenderizers. Use for game animals ONLY. Either will make tough game tender through and through when you sprinkle them on the meat as you would salt, after pricking the meat with a fork to promote penetration. For best results apply when the meat is at room temperature and 30 to 60 minutes before cooking. Neither Accent nor monosodium glutinate has a taste or smell and each is astonishingly effective on game that may not have hung quite long enough.

A FEW SPECIFICS ABOUT GAME

Bears eat berries, fruit, honey and vegetables wherever and whenever they can get them. The meat is rich and savory.

Rabbit and hare meat is much like chicken. The wild species have a slight gamey taste which proper treatment dissipates. (See individual recipes.)

Muskrats live on plants. The meat is delicious when processed like rabbit or hare.

Wild duck, for the most part, feed on wild rice or any marsh grain. Only in some parts of North America do they eat fish. If they have a fishy smell, wash them with a damp cloth, soaked in vinegar water or put into their cavities onion, celery or apple wrapped in bacon. The oil sacs in a duck's tail should be removed carefully.

Pheasant should be hung 4 to 6 days to develop their flavor. The meat is quite dry and should be well larded with bacon or salt pork.

Partridge feed on berries and other fruit including apples as well as wild grain. Hang for at least 4 days.

Quail is also a very dry bird and needs a lot of larding. Eat quail as soon as possible after killing. Do not hang. Should you want to freeze them, do it the same day.

DRESSING AND HANGING

Venison, moose, bear and wild boar must be opened in the field as soon as shot and, with the help of some sticks, kept open so the gas and blood can escape easily. Do not put freshly killed game in the closed trunk of your car or smaller game in a knapsack: keep them exposed so they'll be cool. If game is shot in the evening, particularly on a warm day and is not found until the next morning, all green parts (the discolored ones) are not fit for human consumption unless put into a marinade and cooked right away.

Large game animals with the exception of wild boar need aging. They will be far more tender and better flavored if they are hung, just above freezing, for two weeks or more. Rabbit and other small game should hang 8 to 12 days.

When you hang game never — but never — bring it into contact with water. Only rub it with a clean, dry cloth. The room must be cool, dry, airy and, last but not least, free of flies. To be sure of keeping flies off, wrap it in cheese cloth. If such a room is not available, take your game to your butcher and ask him to hang it in his cold room for you.

Young game is naturally more tender and requires less aging and, in some cases, less cooking than older game. The difference in the meat is obvious to experienced hands: the feel of the flesh and its color tell the story. Young animals' flesh is not as firm or as sinewy as that of mature animals and is generally lighter in color. As to antlered animals, the fewer the points, the younger the beast.

HOW TO SKIN A RABBIT OR HARE AND CLEAN IT

Rabbit or hare should be skinned as soon as possible after being killed and put into a stone crock for 24 hours. To skin, hang the animal by its hind legs and cut off the paws. Then cut around the anus and pull the skin up to the neck and cut off the head. Another way is to cut the skin on the inside of the legs, pull the legs through, slit the skin down the belly, peel back and cut off the head.

Clean the insides only after skinning. Cut open the stomach to the breast bone and take everything out with your hand. Throw away the intestines and the stomach. The heart, liver and kidneys can be used. The gall, next to the liver, must be removed carefully so that it does not break and pour its contents over the liver. Pour the blood that has accumulated into a bowl, add a little vinegar and save it for making a sauce or putting into a ragout.

Remove any remaining hair from the body, cut out the thorax (windpipe), shoulders and neck. The animal is now in a white lining which must be removed with a small, sharp knife, carefully pulling and shaving the meat back. You will note that the meat is now nice and dark. Wrap in a vinegar-soaked cloth if it is young. Otherwise put it into a marinade. (See page 206-7).

HOW TO PREVENT SPOILAGE

When game first comes into the kitchen, you needn't worry about spoilage. But if you plan to keep it a few days, or longer, you'll want to care for it properly.

The most effective way to preserve it is, of course, freezing. It enables you to keep the game as long as you please. In any event, hang the game in a cool room with an even temperature and good ventilation. A draught is good but not necessary. Hang it so that it does not touch anything, not even a wall, so air can circulate around it. Always hang by the neck in order to let blood escape.

When it is cut into roasts, legs, steaks, chops and stew meat, wrap for freezing, mark each package and deposit in your own deep freeze or send it out to a freezer locker. Only freeze the pieces that are in perfect condition: those that have not been badly shot.

A good method for freezing small birds (woodcock, quail, snipe, teal, doves) is in water. This is how I do it: after the birds have been plucked and dressed, push one into a waxed container (milk, ice cream, etc.) fill with water, seal tightly and freeze. It is a wonderful way to keep them moist and the container will not be ripped by small, sharp, outstanding bones as a plastic bag would.

HOW TO TELL THE AGE AND TENDERNESS OF A BIRD

To discover the difference between an old and a young bird (the way and length of time of cooking depends on it) test it this way:

1). Push the end of the breast bone. If it's on the soft side, it's a young bird.

2). The skin on a young bird's feet is lighter in color than an old one's.

3). Young birds have a tiny, pointed pin feather at each wing tip which they lose after the first year. Pull the feather — it should show blood.

4). Young pheasant's tail feathers and spurs are short.

5). Game birds in prime condition are heavy for their size. The breasts are round and firm and the skin clear.

6). Old birds have hard skin on their feet and a hard, inflexible beak.

PLUCKING, CLEANING AND SKINNING BIRDS

Most feathered game must be opened right away and the entrails removed, especially duck, pheasant and partridge if shot on a hot day. Woodcock and snipe need not be cleaned as you can cook them with their entrails intact. Never, but *never* touch feathered game with hot water while cleaning or plucking: it will develop an unpleasant "feathery" taste.

Plucking is not too difficult. Cut off the head, neck, feet and wings. Sit down (if possible outdoors), place a paper bag between your legs, pinning it to your skirt or apron with two safety pins. Start pulling feathers out from the neck down. Always pull upward so you won't tear the meat. Singe off the last small pin feathers over a gas flame or with a candle. (Incidentally, the multi-colored feathers of some game birds are salable, sometimes for a fairly good price. They're used in making hats and fishing flies and have to be collected neatly and protected against moths.)

Water fowl and young crows are not plucked but skinned. Cut carefully up to the breast bone and pull the skin off like a jacket. It is better to skin them before cleaning inside.

Drawing or removing the entrails is done this way: Make a cut from the anus to the lower part of the breast bone. Place your hand inside, close it over the entrails and pull them out. This should remove most of them but, to make sure, thrust your hand in again and pull out the rest, if any. Now put your hand into the neck opening and remove the windpipe and crop. Before cooking wash the cavity thoroughly and dry as thoroughly.

The proper skinning of birds is important. When roasted they will brown nicely and the meat will be tender and free of sinews. To skin, loosen the skin with the left hand and with a small, sharp knife, shave and pull slowly so the meat will be hurt as little as possible. After skinning smooth down the meat with a broad knife. Remove fat, if there is any, as it spoils the taste.

CLEANING AND SCALING FISH

Fish should always be very fresh. To clean, cut open the belly from head to tail, remove the entrails carefully so as not to disturb the gall and liver. These have a bitter taste which can make the fish unpalatable if they permeate the flesh. If cooked with the head on be sure to pull out the gills. Wash inside and out with cold water and dry with a clean cloth or paper towels.

One way to scale a fish is to place it on a board and, using the blunt side of a knife, rub against the scales. I have found that scaling them under water is far better: it keeps the scales from jumping all over the kitchen.

If you don't want to eat the fish right away, *do not* wash with water. Just dry inside and out and put into the refrigerator wrapped in foil or plastic. If you want to keep it longer, put it into the freezer. Fish freezes well and loses very little of its goodness in the process.

Of incidental intelligence: the silvery blue color of trout and salmon can be brought back by pouring one cup of hot, diluted vinegar over them. Makes them look nicer.

SEASONINGS

I am a confirmed "seasoner" and user of herbs. But never do I season or herb dishes to disguise basic flavors. Seasoning, as you know, is designed to accent foods, not dominate them.

Every recipe in this book mentions kinds that contribute to perfecting the finished *pièces de résistance*. While much of my preparing and cooking is by instinct, I have tried to give you exact measurements. They suit me and my husband. You may want to vary them here and there to satisfy your own taste buds.

In earlier days, before the deep freeze, cooks had to use more and stronger spices because the game, whether they liked it or not, was liable to be too "ripe." Today, with aging completely controlled and game preserved in its prime state for months on end in freezers, high seasoning is no more necessary than it is with domestic meats and fowls.

LARDING

Larding of large game, with salt pork or bacon, is a *must* because the meat is dry and has little or no fat. Whichever you use it should be good and cold when you cut it into strips, all the same length and as long as possible.

A larding needle is helpful in pushing the larding into the meat — always with the grain and in even rows. You can lard with hard cheese or anchovy fillets for flavor but always lard at least half of the meat with the salt pork or bacon.

For smaller game — rabbit, hare, muskrat, squirrel, birds —cover with large, thin slices of bacon or salt pork, enough to envelop the breasts. Fasten with string or skewers. Sometimes you will want to lard fish when broiling or baking it. Don't cover the entire surface. Separating the strips by their own width is a safe rule.

GARNISHING FOR MEATS

Always garnish just before you serve so that the garnish will be fresh and attractive. Remember, your guests eat with their eyes as well as their palates. Satisfy both!

Parsley, being perky and of luscious color, is probably the most used garnish. Keep fresh parsley in the refrigerator in a covered glass jar. Do not wash before storing — it will keep crisper and longer.

Watercress and lettuce leaves are particularly good with cold meats. Tomato wedges, hard boiled eggs, radishes cut in "roses," olives and some fancy cut vegetables are nice decorations too.

Even so, don't let your imagination run too wild: the garnish should not overpower. Like a woman's hat it is designed to complement — and compliment — appearance, not supplant natural attractiveness.

GARNISHING FOR SOUPS

Clear soups call for more garnishing than thick soups. For consommés and bouillons, sprinkle with parsley or chopped watercress. Grated cheese, lemon slices, cooked vegetables cut into fancy shapes (carrots, beets, etc.) are good too.

A large spoonful of grated cheese on a small square of toast transforms a consommé into something special. Place squares of toast in the soup, then spoon the grated cheese on them — Swiss, cheddar, parmesan, romano.

Croutons are often used. Brown ½ inch cubes of stale bread either in butter or oil, drain and put into soup. Or place a bowl of them on the table and let your guests help themselves.

MARINADES AND SAUCES

These add much flavor and piquancy to certain kinds of game. For practical reasons — specific recipes and cooking instructions — they are included in Chapter VIII. In some cases they are mentioned and/or detailed under particular game recipes. All are listed in the index for your convenience.

WINES

Wines for cooking should be selected as thoughtfully as those for drinking. You use so little — use the best available! I have specified vintage wines in many recipes not because of "wine snobbery" but because I have found, through experience, that they give more character to food than lesser pressings.

As to what wine to serve with what food, I am not a strict conformist. While I generally serve red wine with meat and white wine with fish and poultry, I have often switched without disastrous results. An excellent "middle of the road" solution is a good rosé: it goes with anything.

FOUR-LEGGED GAME

VENISON

It's my guess that venison is the game in biggest supply
— that deer is the quarry of more hunters than any other of the
larger game animals. And, I might add, it's the most rewarding to prepare and eat. Versatile venison, I call it. Let it
be remembered, however, that moose meat can be prepared and
served the same ways.

When well hung, venison does not need much cooking:
it dries out quickly if over-cooked. Many recipes specify
marinating: there are a number of different marinades. (See
individual recipes as well as the marinades listed separately on
page 206). However, if a specific recipe does not require a
marinade, wrap the meat in a vinegar-soaked cloth. Keep it
wrapped in the refrigerator for 8 days, dampening the cloth
every 2 or 3 days. Another method of conditioning it — which
I prefer — is to put the meat into buttermilk for from 1 to 4
days. Turn it every 12 hours.

Be careful with spices. Venison has a very delicate flavor that should be preserved, not disguised. Herbs like marjoram, thyme and rosemary, used sparingly, or a specially prepared game seasoning are fine. Go easy on the pepper. And never use paprika or caraway seeds: they have too strong individualities.

Following are my favorite ways of preparing and serving venison — enough recipes, I venture, to cook a whole deer without repeating!

VENISON LIVER

In Germany and Austria the killing of a deer is followed by a simple ceremony, participated in by the hunter and the guide. The latter cuts an oak twig (long a symbol of strength), dips it in the deer's blood and, with a deep bow, presents it to the hunter who places it in his hatband as evidence, upon reaching home, that he has shot his quarry.

Traditionally, the liver is the hunter's reward for his prowess — and a much coveted one. For it is a great delicacy that must be removed from the deer as soon as possible and eaten the same day.

This is my favorite way of serving it. You will need these ingredients:

1 venison liver	*¼ cup red wine*
3 tablespoons butter	*Mushrooms (a few)*
1 onion, minced	*1 teaspoon lemon juice*
1 tablespoon flour	*Salt and a dash of pepper*

Melt the butter in a skillet and sauté the minced onion until golden brown. Put in the slices of liver and cook each side for 1½ minutes (no longer or the liver will become tough). Remove liver from skillet and keep warm. Sprinkle the flour into the pan and brown lightly. Add the wine and the finely chopped mushrooms and simmer until thickened. Add the lemon juice, salt and pepper as it nears completion. Put the liver back and warm briefly in the gravy.

VENISON STEAKS OR CHOPS

Spread small steaks (1½ inches thick) or chops with butter and sear in the broiler for a moment or two on each side. Reduce the heat and turn the meat often until it is cooked to suit you. It will take 12 minutes for a rare steak, up to 30 minutes for well done. Chops, if they are thinner, should be cooked less.

Serve them with a sauce made of 4 tablespoons of melted butter, ½ teaspoon salt, ⅛ teaspoon pepper, some finely chopped parsley, a teaspoon of lemon juice and 3 tablespoons of dry sherry.

PLAIN ROAST VENISON

Trim an 8 to 10 pound haunch or, better still, the saddle if you don't mind not having the cutlets. Lard well with strips of bacon or salt pork. You can use a larding needle or if this is too much work, place the strips over the meat, securing them with skewers. Place the meat in a roasting pan in a hot oven (450 degrees). Baste the meat every ten minutes with claret. At the end of ½ hour, reduce the heat to 375 degrees, cover and cook for another two hours. (Altogether allow 20 minutes to the pound).

When done place the meat on a hot platter, sprinkle some flour in the drippings and stir until blended. Add some sour cream to the gravy — it adds zest.

Serve with currant or wild plum jelly.

MARINATED ROAST VENISON

Either the haunch or saddle will do. The meat should stand in the marinade for several days before roasting.

To make the *marinade* you will need:

2 cups vinegar	*2 bay leaves*
2 cups water	*4 onions, chopped*
4 cloves	*Salt, Pepper*

Combine the vinegar, water, onions, spices and boil briefly. Pour HOT over the meat and let it stand in the refrigerator for several days.

FOR ROASTING

6 tablespoons melted	*Bacon slices*
butter	*1 tablespoon lemon juice*
6 tablespoons bacon fat	*3 tablespoons flour*
from bacon slices or oil	*2 cups vintage red wine*
2 cups sour cream	*(optional)*

Wipe the meat dry and brown on all sides in the melted butter and bacon fat or oil. Cover with bacon slices. Pour over some of the marinade with the onions, cover the roasting pan tightly and roast at 375 degrees until meat is done — about 15 minutes per pound. Baste frequently. Uncover the last half hour to let the meat brown nicely. Place on warm platter and keep hot.

Now add to the pan juices the flour, lemon juice, sour cream and, if you choose, wine. Stir constantly until it thickens and smooths out. Strain and pour over the meat or serve it separately. Noodles and cranberries go well with it. 6 to 10 servings, depending on size of the roast.

ROAST SADDLE OF VENISON AND GRAVY

Here's another way of roasting. There's no marinade in-
volved. If the meat hasn't been skinned it will be up to
you to do it. It goes without saying it should be well
hung. Remove any sinews and trim the ribs to give the
roast more eye appeal. Rub all over with salt and pepper,
then wrap it in cheesecloth soaked with vinegar or red
wine, letting it stand overnight. Or pour buttermilk over
it and let it stand the same length of time.

6 or 7 pounds venison   1 onion
    saddle   1 cup sour cream
Bacon strips   1 lemon
6 tablespoons butter   2 tablespoons flour
2 cups boullion or   Salt and pepper
    beef stock

When cooking time comes around, dry the meat, cover
with bacon strips and roast in melted butter and sliced
onion for 10 or 15 minutes in a 450 degree oven. Then
moisten with bouillon or beef stock and roast, covered,
in 350 degree oven. When nearly done (allowing 10 minutes per pound), lift cover and baste often until meat is
brown. At the last minute spoon some of the sour cream
over it and leave in oven a few minutes more. The total
cooking time will be about one hour and twenty minutes:
the meat should be rosy pink.

Now carve the fillets from the underside of the saddle (carve at an angle from the bone) and rearrange on the platter with the carved slices on top. Garnish with lemon slices with the rind removed. Serve the gravy separately.

To make the gravy: Sprinkle flour in the pan in which the meat was roasted, add lemon juice, water or consommé, the rest of the sour cream and a small amount of red wine. Stir constantly until thickened and smooth.

It's nice with mashed potatoes and you'll want some currant jelly. Serves 8.

COLD SADDLE OF VENISON

Follow the preceding recipe but cook the saddle a little less than you would to serve it hot — the meat should be pinker inside. Carve as above and garnish with lemon slices and little bouquets of parsley. Top each lemon slice with ½ teaspoon of red currant jelly. Serve with Cold Orange Sauce or Cumberland Sauce (pages 202, 206). Serves 8, at least.

LARDED SADDLE OF VENISON

See recipe for Larded Saddle of Hare, page 66.

GRILLED FILLET OF VENISON

2 pounds venison fillets　　　*¾ cup olive oil*
4 or 5 slices fat bacon　　　*Salt and pepper*
　　or salt pork　　　　　　*Small gherkins*

Cut fillets into ½ or ¾ inch thick slices, lard with bacon, rub with salt and pepper. Pour oil over meat and turn from time to time so the oil can penetrate.

Broil 3 to 5 minutes on each side. Garnish with gherkins. Serve with potatoes, noodles or wild rice and a piquant sauce such as Béarnaise, Sauce Espagnol or Cold Orange Sauce (pages 197 and 202). 4 Servings.

MARINATED FILLETS OF VENISON

For the marinade:

¾ cup of vinegar   *4 shallots, sliced*
1 bay leaf   *1 clove*
1 sprig thyme   *A little parsley*
2 small onions, sliced   *Salt and pepper*

Cook the vinegar together with the other ingredients for 5 minutes, then strain through a sieve. Cut the fillets into thin slices and let them stand in the marinade in a cool place for one hour.

For Cooking:

2 pounds venison fillets   *1 cup consommé or stock*
4 to 6 tablespoons   *1 teaspoon flour*
     butter   *1 teaspoon butter*
5 tablespoons cognac

Pat the meat dry and brown both sides quickly in the melted butter. Remove from skillet and place in pyrex or other heatproof serving dish. Pour the cognac into the pan in which the fillets were browned. Add the marinade, consommé, flour and teaspoon of butter. Stir until dissolved and boiling. Pour over the fillets and simmer until done (about 15 minutes). Serve with purée of chestnuts (see page 212) or baked apple slices. 4 to 6 servings.

VENISON STROGANOFF A LA BARBARA

This is an elegant dish for a party, one I have served
many times with unvarying success. It can be prepared
the day before — some claim it's better when reheated.
I agree. (Moose steaks are equally good.)
For 4 to 6 servings:

4½ pounds venison steak	*3 tablespoons butter*
½ pound mushrooms, halved	*½ pint sour cream*
	1 tablespoon flour
	Salt and pepper

Cut the steaks into 1 inch strips, ¼ inch thick. If possible cut *across* the grain as it makes the meat even more
tender. Melt the butter in a heavy skillet and cover. When
the butter is bubbling add the meat and cook slowly, covered. Stir occasionally. After 15 minutes add the mushrooms. Cover and cook another 10 minutes.

Now put the meat and mushrooms into the top of a double boiler over low heat. (Keep the water in the bottom
well below the upper section). Melt 1 more tablespoon
of butter in the skillet, add the flour, stirring constantly
until smooth. Add the sour cream and stir over very low
heat for 3 or 4 minutes: it should not boil.

Finally, pour the sauce over the meat and mushrooms in
the double boiler and simmer for 10 or 15 minutes. Season to taste with salt and pepper.

Serve in a ring of noodles or boiled rice. Have French
bread ready to sop up the sauce. Currant jelly and a
crisp green salad are excellent accompaniments. My taste
runs to Caesar Salad or the He-Man Salad (see page
190).

If you are serving buffet style, put the Stroganoff into
a chafing dish and let your guests help themselves.

IZAAK HUNTER'S VENISON OR MOOSE STROGANOFF

My friend, Izaak Hunter, Editor of the Rod and Gun column in the Montreal *Gazette*, is not only a great sportsman but also an epicure who has developed a number of
notable game recipes. This is one of his best, a bit more
complicated to prepare than my Stroganoff, but emi-
nently worth while.

2 pounds steak	*1 tablespoon tomato paste*
5 tablespoons butter	*5 tablespoons sour cream,*
2 tablespoons flour	*scalded*
1 can beef consommé	*½ teaspoon ground chervil*
or bouillon	*2 tablespoons grated onion*

Salt and pepper

Cut the 2 pounds of steak into 1 inch cubes. Sprinkle generously with salt and freshly ground black pepper and let stand in a cool place for 2 or 3 hours.

When you are ready to put the dish together melt 2 tablespoons of butter in a skillet, blend in 2 tablespoons of flour over low heat, stirring constantly until it is reduced to a brown paste. Stir in 1 can of beef consommé or bouillon and cook — still stirring — until smooth. Strain into a sauce pan and bring to a boil. Remove from heat and stir in 1 tablespoon of tomato paste, 5 tablespoons of scalded sour cream and ½ teaspoon of ground chervil. Bring gradually to a boil and let it simmer while you prepare the meat.

Cook the meat in the skillet in 3 tablespoons of butter and 2 tablespoons of grated onion over high heat. When the meat is delicately browned, season the sauce to taste and add the meat to it. Simmer for 20 minutes.

Serve at once, garnishing the platter with triangles of bread fried in butter until crisp and brown, sprinkle finely chopped parsley over the meat. Serves 4 to 6.

This recipe, using fillets of beef is equally enticing.

FILET MIGNON OF VENISON, HUNTER STYLE

Have 3 pounds of venison from the leg or loin cut into steaks about ¾ inch thick. Season with salt. Place in a bowl. Prepare a *marinade* made of

½ cup white wine   *½ teaspoon thyme*
1 medium onion, sliced   *4 sprigs parsley*
1 carrot, diced   *1 bay leaf*
                  5 tablespoons olive oil

Mix ingredients and pour over steaks. Cover and put into refrigerator for 24 hours. Turn the meat from time to time.

When ready to cook, remove the meat from the marinade and pat dry. Heat 3 tablespoons of olive oil in a skillet.

Fry the steaks 3 minutes on each side — longer if you want them well done. Remove meat to warm serving dish and keep hot while you make a sour cream sauce (see page 201). Try this with purée of lentils (see page 213) and red cabbage (see page 210). 4 servings.

VENISON "SCHNITZEL"

This is not even a remote relative of Wiener Schnitzel but I think you'll like it as I do, name and all.

4 large slices venison	*2 tomatoes*
haunch	*1 onion chopped*
4 tablespoons butter	*1 teaspoon flour*
	Red wine

Heat the butter in a large skillet. Add the tomatoes, cut in half, and the chopped onion. Fry the meat in this mixture until it is golden brown on both sides (about 10 minutes). Remove to a warm serving plate and garnish with the tomatoes.

In the same skillet stir together flour, salt, pepper and a small portion of red wine. Cook until smooth then put through a sieve and pour over the meat. 4 servings.

VENISON STEW

I'm including two ways of making venison stew. This one calls for marinating, the second one doesn't. Both are excellent ways of preparing venison shoulder meat, a cut that is not as tender as the saddle or haunch.

For the marinade:

½ cup vinegar	*1 clove*
½ cup water	*1 chopped onion*
1 bay leaf	*Salt and pepper*

Cut the meat into 1 inch squares and place in a deep dish. Pour over the marinade and let it stand in the refrigerator for several days.

The Stew:

3 pounds venison shoul-	2 tablespoons melted
der, cut into 1 inch	butter
cubes	4 tablespoons flour
2 slices bacon or salt	1 cup vintage red wine
pork	Juice of ½ lemon
1 sliced onion	Salt and pepper

Cut the bacon or salt pork into squares and fry with the onion in a large skillet. Add the meat and brown on all sides.

In a Dutch oven or large pot mix melted butter, flour, wine and lemon juice. Add the meat together with enough water or consomme to cover. Put in the seasonings, the lemon juice and the wine. Simmer for 3 hours.

To serve, put the meat into a deep serving dish and cover with the sauce, previously strained through a sieve. Dumplings are an extra added attraction you'll like. 4 to 6 servings.

SWABIAN VENISON STEW

Swabia is in the southwest part of Germany where the Black Forest is. Long ago it was a Duchy, one of the richest and most civilized in Germany. The court was famous for its gay and colorful life. Musicians, painters and authors added much to the culture and the cuisine was excellent.

Here is a sample — a dish of notable stature, truly fit for Kings:

3 pounds venison shoul-
    der cut into 1 inch
    cubes
4 tablespoons butter
4 tablespoons flour
4 cups hot water
1 whole onion studded
    with 2 cloves
        6 peppercorns

2 cups bouillon
1½ teaspoons salt
Juice of ½ lemon
1 cup red wine
2 tablespoons capers
    (optional)
1 bay leaf
½ cup sour cream

Pat the meat dry. Heat butter in a deep pot or Dutch oven.

Stir in the flour and cook until brown. Add hot water, boullion and salt, stirring until well blended and smooth.

Add the peppercorns, the onion studded with cloves and the bay leaf. Boil for 5 minutes.

Now put in the meat, cover and simmer for 1½ hours.

Add the wine and lemon juice and simmer for another 15 minutes. If the sauce becomes too thick add more bouillon.

When the meat is done, remove the onion and bay leaf.

Taste and add more salt, if needed, and plenty of black pepper. Finally stir in ½ cup of sour cream and, if needed, a little more lemon juice or wine until you're satisfied the flavor is piquant enough.

If you choose to add the capers, put them in when you add the wine and lemon juice. 6 servings.

VENISON RAGOUT A LA MONTCALM

You'll have to keep the meat in a marinade in the refrigerator or a cool place for a week. It's worth the wait: the finished property has real character!

The recipe calls for 4 to 5 pounds of venison shoulder. Wipe the meat with a wet cloth. Cut into 1½ inch cubes.

Place in an enamelled kettle or large crock and cover with a mixture of equal parts vinegar and red wine. Add 2 sliced onions, 2 diced carrots, 6 peppercorns, 2 bay leaves and a tablespoon of salt.

When ready, a week later, drain the meat. Melt suet or lard in a heavy, very hot roasting pan. Brown the venison quickly in a very hot oven that has been preheated to 475-500 degrees. Add the onions and carrots from the marinade (do not use the liquid). Put in 1 cup of red wine and enough water to cover the meat. Lower heat to 350 degrees — or just hot enough to simmer the liquid in the pan. Cook for 2½ to 3 hours. Remove any excess fat and place meat on a hot serving dish. Keep warm.

Stir enough flour into the pan to make a smooth gravy, bring to a boil on the top of the stove, stirring all the time. Pour over the venison. 6 to 8 servings.

JIM WRIGHT'S CORNED MOOSE

If you have killed a large moose, or if a friend of yours has, and gives you a sizeable chunk — 50 pounds or more of shoulder and/or brisket — here's a different and not particularly difficult way to process and preserve the meat. It's perfectly delicious corned.

You'll need a 10 gallon crock in which to put 5½ pounds of coarse salt, 2½ pounds of sugar, 10 ounces of saltpeter and 4½ gallons of water. Stir until the solids are dissolved. Now add 3 cups of whole mixed pickling spice without cinnamon and 10 or 12 sliced garlic cloves. You'll want to cut the meat into reasonable sizes and thicknesses — 6 to 10 pound pieces.

Put them in the crock and weigh them down with a clean oak or other hardwood board or a clean rock to keep the meat submerged. The length of time for curing depends on the thickness of the meat: approximately 6 days for each inch of thickness. Thus, if the thickest piece is 4 inches, 24 days of curing is called for. The crock should be kept cool — between 38 and 45 degrees — during the curing. When finished remove from the solution and dry with a clean cloth.

Cook as you would corned beef, simmering it in water until tender. Serve it hot or cold. After cooking and cooling it can be stored in the refrigerator for cold cuts. Cover it well with cracked black pepper.

Of course this is a rather sizable project and the amount of meat you will have will be considerable. You can give some of it away or trim your corning to your needs and only cure a small amount — 10 or 15 pounds.

MOOSE STEAK AND MUSHROOMS

Bill Roux had this recipe in his "What's Cooking Down in Maine." As he said "If you've never had moose meat and if, by remote happenstance, some friend of yours brings one down from Canada and gives you a steak, here's one way of cooking it. I found it in a recent Orr's Island cook book."

½ cup finely chopped onion	1 cup chopped mushrooms
2 tablespoons butter	2 tablespoons flour
½ cup sweet or sour cream	

Fry the onions in the butter until brown. (An iron skillet is best.) Sear the steak on both sides in the browned onions and butter. Cover and simmer for ½ hour. When almost tender add the mushrooms, stir the flour into the cream and add to the meat. Cover and let simmer until done.

Venison or bear steaks would do just as well. Or, for that matter, a beef round steak.

ROAST HERBED HAUNCH OF BEAR

While many people turn up their noses at the idea of bear meat, it is really delicious when well aged and prepared.

The proper preparation starts in the field. If the bear is a male he should be castrated right off just as you would castrate a wild boar, buck deer or wild ram. He should then be carefully skinned, leaving no strands of hair on the meat.

As soon as possible get him to a cold storage locker where he can be finally cleaned, dressed and hung up by his heels to be aged as fine beef is aged. After three weeks of hanging he can either be eaten or frozen for future use. The hind quarters should be cut at the hips and the chops and loins cut for broiling. Use the rest of him for stew meat.

When you're ready to have a bear dinner, invite your guests but don't tell them what kind of meat you are serving until they've eaten it and are well gorged — then make them guess!

If the hind quarter (haunch) has been frozen, thaw it in the refrigerator for 2 days. Take it out and rub well with vinegar. When the vinegar has dried, rub the meat with a mixture of meat tenderizer, ground black pepper, ground rosemary, dried mustard and powdered oregano. (You can powder the rosemary and oregano in a mortar and pestle.) Pound this mixture into the meat, pricking it with a fork to help it get down in. Put it back in the refrigerator overnight.

On the day of the big feast, remove the meat from the refrigerator and let it sit at room temperature for 2½ to 3 hours.

When ready to roast rub all over with butter or margarine and place in a covered roasting pan. Keep about 2 cups of water in the pan all the time it is cooking and baste frequently. Cook in a moderate oven — 300 to 350 degrees — for 1½ hours then turn the meat over and cook for another hour.

If you want bear gravy — and you should! — thicken the cooking juices with flour and, if you wish, add some brandy.

BEAR STEAKS AND CHOPS

These can be prepared and cooked as you cook venison or moose. (See pages 36, 54).

SMOKED HAM OF BEAR OR WILD BOAR

Wild boar is not common in North America. It's too bad because the meat is excellent and can be cooked in the same ways as domestic pork. If you should come across a wild boar, remember he'll have to be inspected by a veterinarian for, like pigs, he's subject to trichinosis.

You may never have occasion to do this but, just in case, here's how to smoke a ham of bear or wild boar.

10 quarts water   3 pounds salt
3 tablespoons sugar

Bring the ingredients to a boil and let cool. Place the ham of bear or wild boar — or for that matter, pig — in a big earthenware crock. Pour the solution over it.

Weight the meat down with a stone or other weight and cover tightly. Turn the ham every second day for three weeks. Then remove and let it drip dry.

Now, if you have a smoke room, put the ham into a synthetic material (plastic) bag and hang it in the smoke for two weeks. Or, do it the easy way, take it to your butcher and ask him to have it done for you.

It's delicious when sliced and eaten uncooked. And, of course, you can roast it or bake it if you prefer.

BARBECUED WILD BOAR RIBS, HAWAIIAN

Get 5 or 6 pounds of meaty boar ribs. (In a pinch pork will do, but don't tell!) Marinate overnight in the refrigerator in a marinade made of

⅓ cup vinegar	*1 level teaspoon*
⅓ cup sherry	*paprika*
⅓ cup soy sauce	*1 level teaspoon salt*
3 tablespoons honey	*1 clove garlic, minced*
1 level teaspoon black	*½ teaspoon ground*
pepper	*ginger*

Before cooking pour the marinade into a jar. Place the ribs in a heavy skillet or iron baking pan and brown in a little butter. Then put it into the oven and bake at 300 to 350 degrees for 1½ hours, basting often with the marinade.

HARES AND RABBITS

Hares and rabbits are members of the same family. There is a biological variance, however, as well as a difference in the character and color of the flesh. The young of the hare are open-eyed and furred at birth while baby rabbits are born naked. And hare meat is on the dark side while rabbit meat is white. Preparation and cooking methods are the same. Use either in the recipes that follow. And if the wild varieties are unavailable, you will find domestic animals in the market.

The best hares are the young ones. A good way to distinguish young from old is by the teeth: young hares have very white, short, sharp teeth; old ones' teeth are dark and dull.

The head, neck, forelegs, shoulders, side parts, heart and lungs can be used in stews. The back or saddle and the hind legs are the best for roasts. Badly shot animals should be used only for stews and ragouts.

JUGGED HARE

Here are three recipes for jugged hare, the first using the rear legs and the saddle, the second using everything but the saddle and rear legs and the third, a favorite of Izaak Hunter, featuring snowshoe hare. As Mr. Hunter says, "Of the almost countless ways of preparing the flesh of this intriguing little animal, jugging is one of the best." I agree with him.

METHOD NO. 1

> *2 rear legs and 1 saddle,*   *1 tablespoon lemon*
>   *all cut into 2 pieces*   *juice*
> *1½ teaspoons salt*   *12 peppercorns*
> *7 tablespoons butter*   *1 herb bouquet (pars-*
> *1 medium size onion*   *ley, thyme and bay*
> *4 cloves*   *leaf)*
> *1½ cups port or*   *3 cups hot stock or*
>   *claret wine*   *bouillon*
>   *1 tablespoon flour*

Rinse the meat and pat dry. Rub with salt. Sauté in 3 tablespoons of butter until brown, roughly 30 minutes.

Place in a casserole, add the whole onion studded with cloves, ¾ cup of wine, the lemon juice, peppercorns, herbs and stock. Cover and bake in a moderate oven (350 degrees) for 2½ to 3 hours. About ½ hour before it is done, melt the remaining 4 tablespoons of butter, blend with the flour and stir it into the hot mixture. Add the remaining ¾ cup of wine and any needed seasoning. Re-cover the casserole and cook for ½ hour. 4 servings. (The size of rabbits and hare vary.)

METHOD NO. 2

For this you will want the head, neck, ends of the ribs, forelegs, lungs, liver and heart, cut into 1 inch squares. Make a marinade of the following:

½ cup red wine	*4 whole peppers*
½ cup water	*1 onion, chopped*
1 clove	*Salt*
1 bay leaf	*Pepper*

Pour the marinade over the meat and let it stand for 2 to 3 days.

When ready to cook, heat 3 or 4 tablespoons of bacon fat, butter or shortening. Fry the meat with minced onion, add 3 to 4 tablespoons of flour and brown with the meat. Put in half of the marinade, cover, and simmer in a 350 degree oven for 2½ to 3 hours. If the juice boils down, add more marinade or water. When ready add the blood of the hare which I hope you have saved. A small glass of sherry, lemon juice and spice will give the right piquancy to the sauce. Serve with noodles or dumplings. 4 servings.

METHOD NO. 3: IZAAK HUNTER'S

1 hare
2 tablespoons melted
* butter*
1 onion, minced
1 clove garlic, mashed
1 bay leaf

1 teaspoon anise seed
1 tablespoon lemon
* juice*
¼ cup bouillon
⅛ teaspoon pepper
½ teaspoon salt

½ teaspoon marjoram

Carefully wash, trim and dry the hare. Cut into serving pieces, making 3 of the back and 2 of each hind leg. Brown on all sides in butter then put into the top of a double boiler. Add the onion, garlic, bay leaf, lemon juice, bouillon, salt, pepper, marjoram and anise. Cover and simmer for 3 hours. Remove the meat and strain the gravy.

Then thicken the gravy with a tablespoon of flour mixed with a little cold milk. Serve over the meat. 4 servings.

BRAISED LEG OF HARE, CANADIENNE

Hindquarters dressed
hare
6 thin slices bacon
1 cup butter, melted
1½ tablespoons flour

1 cup sour cream
2 tablespoons lemon
juice
1 cup hot water
Salt and pepper

Split the hindquarters lengthwise into 2 pieces. Rinse, drain and pat dry. Rub well with salt and pepper.

Arrange the meat in a baking pan which has been rubbed with bacon fat or oil, then cover with the bacon slices.

Cook in a hot oven (475 degrees) for 25 minutes. Lower the heat to 350 degrees. Baste with the melted butter and continue cooking for another 25 minutes. Sprinkle with flour, smear with sour cream, add the lemon juice and water. Cover and cook for 20 minutes, stirring the pan sauce from time to time. Let the sauce thicken and cook down. Serves 3 or 4.

RACK OF HARE WITH GRAPES

This is a favorite and elegant recipe of Elisabeth, Princess Altenburg of Austria. Make a marinade of

2½ cups water	*1 bay leaf*
½ cup vinegar or wine	*1 teaspoon thyme*
3 sprigs parsley	*1 sliced carrot*
1 clove of garlic	

Marinate the rack for 2 days, turning every 12 hours.

Dry the rack, season with salt and pepper. Place in pan with bacon fat or rub with oil. Cook in 475 degree oven for 45 minutes (or 20 minutes to the pound). Add a glass of brandy and light cream. Baste often, using the strained marinade. Remove rack from pan and keep warm.

Into the pan pour ½ cup of light cream or buttermilk, add 1 teaspoon prepared French mustard and a handful of seedless white grapes. Pour the gravy over the rack and serve immediately. Serves 2 or 3.

ROAST SADDLE OF HARE

1 saddle of hare	*1 cup sour cream*
3 slices fat bacon	*1 tablespoon flour*
3 tablespoons butter	*1 lemon*
1 onion, chopped	*Salt and pepper*

Lard the meat with bacon strips using a larding needle (see page 26). Or place whole slices over the meat, fastening them with toothpicks.

Melt butter and brown the meat. Add the chopped onion, cover and roast in a 375 degree oven, allowing 20 minutes per pound. Baste every 5 minutes, as the meat tends to be dry. 10 minutes before it is done, take the cover off, pour over the sour cream and place on a platter in a warm oven.

Garnish with lemon slices.

Make gravy in the roasting pan by adding flour, lemon juice and salt and pepper. Serve with red cabbage and cranberries. 4 servings.

LARDED SADDLE OF HARE (OR VENISON)

1 saddle of hare or	*6 slices bacon or salt*
venison	*pork*
1 clove garlic	*Sour cream sauce*
3 tablespoons butter	*(see page 201)*
2½ teaspoons salt	*Orange slices*
⅛ teaspoon cayenne	*Currant jelly*

Rinse the meat and pat dry. Leave it whole or cut into 4 pieces, as you prefer. Rub all over with garlic then butter. (Omit the garlic, if you wish. The meat's delicate gamey flavor is delightful without it.) Sprinkle with salt, and cayenne. Lard or cover with the bacon or salt pork. Place in roasting pan and roast uncovered in a 350 degree oven, allowing 20 minutes per pound. When done remove to a serving platter and keep warm.

Make the sour cream sauce in the pan from which the meat has been removed. Cover the meat and garnish with orange slices. Currant jelly and wild rice are delicious with this. Serves 4.

HARE CHARTREUSE

A favorite of the Order of Catholic Monks at the Monastery of Chartreuse near Grenoble, for which they should be as famous as they have been for the green and white liqueurs they've been making for many, many years. It is a casserole dish and it's *that* good!

There are several steps in its preparation. The meat must be de-boned and cut into bite size squares, then larded with bacon. (See below for cooking). You will have to make a farce or filling. Then there are two steps in cooking. Here are the ingredients you will need:

1 rack of hare and the hind legs	*2 tablespoons flour*
	3 tablespoons fat
Salt and pepper	*Bouillon stock or water*
4 slices bacon	*1 tablespoon Madeira wine*

To line the casserole:

1 parsley or celery root	*2 small cabbages*
	Boiled, sliced carrots

For the Farce (or Filling):

1 tablespoon butter	*¼ cup milk*
1 pinch nutmeg	*1 egg yolk*
Salt and pepper	*Meat of hare's neck, minced*

2 tablespoons butter to grease casserole

First the larded pieces of hare should be seasoned with salt and pepper, rolled in flour and browned slightly in the hot fat. Add the soup stock or water and the Madeira wine and simmer until soft.

While this is simmering, make the farce. (The meat should be fixed in advance). Beat the butter, salt, pepper, nutmeg, milk and egg yolk until foamy. Add the minced meat.

Now grease the casserole and line with slices of boiled carrots and sliced parsley or celery root. Cover the bottom with the farce. Blanch the cabbage leaves, roll them around the browned meat and put them into the casserole. Place additional cabbage leaves on top. Cook in a 350 degree oven for 1 hour. 4 generous servings.

RABBIT A LA HOLIDAY

Allow ¾ pound of rabbit per person. Disjoint rabbit into 5 segments: 2 hindquarters, 1 center saddle, 2 forequarters. Rub each piece with salt and pepper and butter and put into a shallow roasting pan in which you have poured 1½ cups of water. Cover and cook slowly in a 350 degree oven for 1½ hours. 10 minutes before serving remove cover and brown in hot oven.

Place rabbit, well garnished, in a serving dish and pour over Holiday Sauce (see page 198).

RABBIT, SOUTHERN STYLE

1 rabbit	*1 or 2 eggs*
Salt and pepper	*1 cup flour*
Lemon juice	*Shortening*

Cut the rabbit into serving pieces and rub with salt, pepper and lemon juice. Dip the meat in beaten egg, roll in the flour and fry in deep hot fat until golden brown. (If the rabbit is not too young, parboil it in simmering salted water for 10 minutes, dry off and then rub with salt, pepper and lemon juice. Let stand for an hour. Then proceed as above.)

Serve with potato or green salad, peas or green beans.

SQUIRRELS

Although they are not hunted widely in Europe, squirrels are popular game in Canada and the United States. Squirrel meat, especially that of the gray squirrel, is perfectly delicious when properly prepared and cooked. The flesh is light red or pink and the gamey flavor is not too pronounced. Young animals are best fried, grilled or baked. The older and tougher need to be stewed for best results.

BAKED SQUIRREL

Allow at least ½ squirrel per person. To halve them split them down the back. Bake the halved sections, cavity down, in a roasting pan. Sprinkle with salt and pepper and pour over each some melted butter. Add the water and cook very slowly — at 250 degrees — for about 2 hours.

When they are fork tender, remove from pan and keep warm. Make gravy by adding a mixture of flour and water to the pan juices and simmer on top of the stove, stirring constantly, until it is the consistency you want.

BOOMER À LA MARYLAND

In the Smoky Mountains there are a number of types of squirrels including the fox squirrel (very large), the grey squirrel and the red squirrel which the natives call "Boomer." It is a small squirrel and a mouth-watering morsel.

Quarter each squirrel and dredge all pieces in flour seasoned with salt and pepper. Brown over medium heat in a skillet, using salad oil or other frying fat. (Bacon drippings suit me best.) When well browned on both sides, pour in 2 cups of water and simmer very gently with a tight lid on the skillet. Test for tenderness: they're done when fork tender. Add more water while cooking if necessary.

NEW BRUNSWICK STEW

This stew is not indigenous to New Brunswick. According to Frank Shay, author of THE BEST MEN ARE COOKS, "Every Brunswick, from Canada to Georgia and clear across the Atlantic to Germany, has laid claim to creating this delectable dish. Careful research reveals that it was originally pulled together in Brunswick County, Virginia." Today chicken and rabbit are the meat bases more often than squirrels. Thus if squirrels are unavailable, substitute. Either way you'll produce a great stew. The New Brunswick method differs primarily from others in that the meat is not browned first.

2 *squirrels*
6 *ounces corn, cut*
from cob
2 *medium potatoes,*
diced
6 *ounces lima beans*
1 *pound tomatoes,*
quartered

¼ *onion chopped*
4 *pints boiling water*
¼ *teaspoon sage*
1 *bay leaf*
1½ *teaspoons sugar*
1½ *teaspoons salt*
½ *teaspoon pepper*
3 *ounces butter*

Cut the squirrels into 6 or 7 pieces. Into the boiling water put the squirrel meat, corn, lima beans, tomatoes, potatoes, sugar, onion, salt, pepper, sage and bay leaf. Cover the pot and simmer for 2 hours. Then add the butter and simmer for 10 minutes. At the last bring it to a boil and quickly remove from stove. Serve at once. 3 to 4 servings.

MISCELLANEOUS GAME ANIMALS

MUSKRAT LOUISIANA

The muskrat, believe it or not, is delectable. And this comparatively simple way of preparing and cooking the little animal brings out the best in him. Allow ½ muskrat per person.

Clean thoroughly, after skinning and removing the head and tail. Be sure to remove the musk glands or pouch and trim all fat under the leg pits. This is a MUST!

In an appropriately sized bowl add 4 tablespoons of vinegar to a pint and a half of cold water and put in the muskrat. Store in the refrigerator overnight.

The next day cut up the animal as you would a rabbit: 2 hindquarters, the saddle and 2 forequarters. Roll each piece in flour, seasoned with salt and pepper, and pan fry in bacon drippings or other fat until all sides are browned. Then add two cups of water and simmer in the covered skillet until the meat is fork tender.

Prepare yourself for a surprise: you have a real treat in store!

ROAST POSSUM WITH GRAVY, TAR HEEL STYLE

Brer Possum is grand eating if you have an open mind and the fortitude to dispel thoughts of his somewhat unsavory appetite and his rat-like tree swinging.

To prepare him (assuming he has not been dressed) dip him in a pot of boiling water to which have been added a cup or two of wood ashes from your fireplace. Let him soak for about half a minute then scrape off the fur with a scraping knife. He will be as white and pretty as a young, scraped suckling pig. (Never skin a possum).

Now proceed to clean him inside and sever his head and tail.

Place him on his tummy in a roasting pan and half cover with water. Salt and pepper well and throw in 1 bay leaf and a quartered orange. Cover tightly and roast at 300 degrees. At the end of 1¼ hours turn the chicken-killing rascal over on his back and roast for another hour and a quarter. Be sure to skim off the fat* every 30 or 35 minutes.

Remove from roasting pan and garnish with flora of your choice. Skim off any fat that's left in the pan and thicken with flour which has first been browned. Baked yams or sweet potatoes are proper accompaniments. 1 possum will serve 2.

*You might save the fat you've skimmed off.
Makes a good chest rub for colds and is also a good scalp tonic!

ROAST BEAVER

4 pounds beaver meat   *1 pound bacon fat or*
                                 suet

Wash and dry the meat well. Place in a roasting pan. Add the fat and roast in 450 degree oven for 20 minutes. Reduce heat to 325 degrees and continue cooking for 30 minutes per pound — in this case 2 hours. Serve with bread sauce (see page 199) or horseradish sauce (see page 205). 4 servings.

ROAST RACCOON

The raccoon is a clean little animal and its meat is particularly good when properly prepared. It is recommended that he be completely skinned and cleaned and refrigerated for at least 24 hours before cooking. Before putting him into the refrigerator rub the outside of the meat and the cavity with black pepper and summer savory.

Now to cook. Place the raccoon back down in a roasting pan in which 4 cups of water and 4 tablespoons of cider vinegar have been poured. Salt and pepper again. Cover the pan and put into a 350 degree oven. After an hour take out of the oven and pour off the accumulated fat. Turn over on his stomach, add more water if necessary, and cook for another hour at 350 degrees.

Serve on a platter garnished with sliced oranges, quartered apples and either fresh mint leaves or sprigs of parsley. Serve with green beans, au gratin potatoes, a light tossed salad and corn bread. A medium size raccoon is about right for 4 people.

GROUND HOG (WHISTLE PIG) AND PORCUPINE

Both of these fat rascals are good eating, prepared as below. The ground hog, of course, is not as difficult to clean as his first cousin, Porky, but that's your problem.

I'm only going to tell you how to cook him after you've done the dirty work!

With a sharp knife skin off as much of the outside fat and cavity fat as you can. Place in a deep pan and cover with cold water. To the water add 1 cut up lemon, ½ cup of mixed pickling spices and 1 cup of vinegar. Cover and simmer slowly for about 2 hours. The meat should be medium tender but not falling off the bone. Pour off any fat accumulation at intervals while cooking.

Remove from the cooking water and place in a roasting pan, cavity down. Pour over orange juice and season well with black pepper and garlic salt. Roast in a hot oven until nicely browned. 1 animal will serve 2.

LARDED HEART OF GAME

For this you can use the heart of deer, moose, wild boar or large hare. Cut open the heart, wash well and either lard or wrap it in bacon strips. Season with salt, pepper, a little pimento and ground ginger. Cook in fat in a skillet. If the heart is unusually large cut it in half. The larger it is the longer it takes to become fork tender. When cooked, cut into slices.

In the same pan make a gravy of herbs, capers or anchovy paste with sour cream or buttermilk or red wine and pour over the slices. The number of servings depends on the size of the heart. Generally speaking ½ pound of meat is a good serving.

SOUR-SWEET LUNGS

Cook the lungs of deer, moose or wild boar in 4 tablespoons of vinegar per quart of salted water for 20 minutes. Let cool and cut into small strips. Prepare a brown sauce using some of the vinegar and water (see page 208).

Put in the lung strips and season with a bay leaf, salt, a little vinegar, grated onion, 1 or 2 juniper berries *or* 1 teaspoon of gin, a dash of sugar *or* syrup of raspberries and a bouillon cube. Heat and serve with rice or noodles.

Here again the size of the lungs will determine the number of servings. Allow ½ pound per person.

GAME TONGUE

The tongue of deer, moose or other big game can be used.

Boil in salted water until fork tender. Skin.

Make a brown sauce using red wine or Madeira. Season to taste with lemon juice, a little sugar, salt and pepper or Praise Allah seasoning (see page 132), and (optional) capers or minced dill pickles.

Cut the hot tongue in slices and pour the sauce over them.

Serve with rice, noodles or spaghetti. 2 to 3 servings.

PILAFF OF GAME

Cut raw game into 1 to 2 inch cubes. (Deer, moose, bear, boar or hare). To ¾ cup of red wine add ¼ cup of oil and 1 leek. Pour cold over the meat and let it stand overnight, covered.

Next day dry the meat. Remove the leek. Brown on all sides in butter and slowly add the red wine and oil marinade. Cook until done (your fork will tell you). The age of the game will largely determine the cooking time.

About 20 or 30 minutes before it is done add some ketchup and cook until done to your liking. Season to taste, adding salt only when finished. 2½ to 3 pounds serves 6 people.

WILD GAME CHILI

Grind up tougher cuts of moose, deer or other four footed game. I promise you a really good chili con carne!

You'll need 2 pounds of meat. Pour 2 tablespoons of cooking oil into your skillet, crumble in the meat. Add 1 finely sliced garlic clove. Cook slowly, breaking up any lumps, until the meat has a grayish color. Now add 3 cups of water and simmer slowly, tightly covered for an hour. If you lose too much water, add more while cooking.

When the meat is tender, salt and pepper to taste, add 3 heaping teaspoons of good chili powder and 1 heaping teaspoon of comino, ground or seed.

If you like a bright red chili, add 2 heaping teaspoons of Spanish paprika. If you want a deep red chili, add a small amount of caramel color or one of the gravy makers.

Thicken with corn meal or flour, adding slowly . 4 servings.

For chili with beans add a can of kidney or pinto beans.

CATCH-AS-CATCH-CAN STEW

Use any four footed or feathered game that has been too badly shot for roasting. Mix your game if you choose.

Cut the raw meat* into 1 to 1½ inch cubes. Cut out all bones. Sprinkle flour over the meat and brown in a little oil with a generous amount of minced onion. If the meat is very lean, add some bacon or ham squares to it. Pour over some vinegar and water or, better still, some red wine diluted with water. Cook until the meat is tender.

At the last add some diced mushrooms, skinned chunks of tomatoes and a few minced peppers (kernels removed).

An extra added attraction can be cut up, cooked chestnuts. Add a little vinegar, sugar, salt, paprika, a dash of nutmeg and Gravy Brown; it has to be sweet-sour.

*You'll have to judge quantities of ingredients by the amount of meat you have. This is an "on your own catch-as-catch-can" stew.

FEATHERED GAME

WILD DUCK

There are many different kinds of ducks. The teal
(green wing and blue) are particularly nice and delicate but I
also like blacks, mallards, Gris, Whistlers and Blue Bills.
Wood ducks are delicious. However, in most parts of North
America the law limits the bag to one a day. The plumage
of the male is very colorful and the feathers are much sought
after by fishermen who tie their own flies.

The mud hen or *poule d'eau*, easily recognized by its big
head and no web between its toes (other ducks are webbed)
has a fishy, muddy taste which comes from its diet. Most ducks
feed on grain and wild rice and taste fishy only when they have
come from the ocean where they feed on fish. One can detect
this easily by stroking the feathers against the grain and smell-
ing. The *poule d'eau* or other ducks that feed on fish must be
skinned and the top fat removed completely. Then they must
be plunged into boiling water for a minute or two so that all
the fat comes off. Now fill the cavities with washed charcoal or with carrots to reduce the fishy taste and smell —

and roast. When finished remove the charcoal or carrots before serving. Another way of minimizing the fishy flavor is to wrap the ducks in vine leaves and bacon and fill the cavities with celery tops.

Hanging ducks does not help: all water fowl should be cooked right away. If the usually firm, meat on the stomach turns soft and green, throw the bird away. Fermentation, especially on hot days, sets in quickly and you will notice a foul odor entirely different from a fishy smell.

Small ducks make excellent roasts. The female is smaller and more tender than the male which is usually the case with all birds. Old ducks are apt to be dry and tough but are good for stews and pies.

How to carve a duck: Carving a duck is more difficult than most feathered game because the joints are tougher. The choicest pieces are from the breast.

Before carving make sure to remove all the juice from the inside by standing the bird upright and letting it flow out. Add the juice to the sauce.

First remove the legs by making a circular incision where they join the body. Insert the fork in the thigh and lift the leg toward you. Cut through the joint.

Next, insert the fork in the lower part of the carcass to get a good hold on it and carve slices from one side of the breast. Begin at the wing and finish against the breast bone. Do the same on the other side. Cut the legs into 2 portions at the thigh joint.

ROAST WILD DUCK

Canvasbacks, red heads, mallards, teals and black ducks are the choicest as they feed mostly on wild rice, wild celery and natural grasses. A duck will serve 2 people, except for teals which will only serve 1.

Skin, clean and wipe out the inside with a damp cloth.

Brush generously with butter or bacon fat, inside and out.

Sprinkle with salt.

Place in a roasting pan in a 450 degree oven, allowing 12 to 15 minutes cooking time per pound (for larger birds allow 20 minutes). Baste every 5 minutes with ¼ cup melted butter in ½ cup of boiling water.

Cut in half and serve one breast as a portion. Or carve as above. Serve with wild rice, seasoned with butter and cayenne pepper. And a Chambertin wine!

BRAISED WILD DUCK WITH ORANGE

| ⅔ cup stock or bouillon | 1⅓ cups Espagnole sauce (page 197) |
| 2 oranges | ½ lemon |

Braise the bird in the stock and Espagnole sauce until tender. Remove from the pan and keep warm. Skim the sauce, reduce, rub through a sieve and add the juice of 2 oranges and ½ lemon. Now blanch thin strips of rind from an orange and half a lemon. Add to the sauce but do not boil again. Pour over the duck and serve with segments of peeled orange.

IZAAK HUNTER'S WILD DUCK IN YOGURT

Duck, cut in serving pieces	1 teaspoon cummin seeds
1 onion, chopped	1 teaspoon chili powder
1 tomato, cut up	1 teaspoon turmeric powder
1 clove garlic	
1 teaspoon ginger	1 pint yogurt
1 cup water	Salt
⅛ teaspoon coreander seed	Cooking fat

Here's an escape from orthodoxy in preparing wild duck and, like all of Mr. Hunter's recipes, an exceptionally fine production.

Mash the garlic and ginger together in a cup of water.

Fry the duck and onion in fat until browned. Add tomato, coreander, turmeric, cummin, chili and yogurt. Then the garlic-ginger-water mixture. Fry for 5 minutes then cover and simmer for 2 hours. Add water as needed.

WILD GOOSE À LA EDIBLE

1 quart water	*1 cup diced celery*
1 carrot	*1 bay leaf*
1 or 2 onions	*Pinch of thyme*
Salt pork slices	*½ cup gin or beer*
Parsley	*Salt and pepper*

Clean the bird. Puncture under wings with fork or knife and rub with salt and pepper. Place the goose with the onions and carrot in a roasting pan. Pour over 1 quart of boiling water, cover tightly and simmer until the water has evaporated and some of the fat is out (about an hour).

Now pour off the fat, cover the bird with salt pork slices, add a little water, parsley, celery, bay leaf and thyme.

Put the roasting pan, without cover, into a preheated oven (375 degrees) and roast for 2 to 3 hours. Baste often. If the goose is very fat, skim off, and if necessary add a little hot water.

15 minutes before serving pour the gin or beer over it. Remove the bird to a platter, cover with aluminum foil and keep warm in the oven.

Pour off all fat in the pan, add to drippings a little flour and hot water and a couple of tablespoons of port wine.

Simmer for 10 minutes — or until it is the consistency you want — drain and serve very hot with cranberry or apple sauce and wild rice. 1 wild goose will serve 2 to 3.

PHEASANT

This king among game birds is best for eating from late Fall until after Christmas for that's when they're nice and fat. The cock is a spectacular sight, his plumage variegated and irridescent. While the hen is a plain jane compared to him, she is no less desirable for the table. In fact, she is apt to be more tender and succulent. Very young birds have to be eaten right after shooting — no hanging for them. You will notice that the young ones have short, rounded spurs, the breastbone is soft and the fat still white. Older pheasants have yellow fat and meat.

If several pheasants are brought into the kitchen, keep only the ones that are dry and not too badly shot. First remove the entrails, then hang the birds by a loop cord around the neck. They can be hung — if it is cool — for one week. When you pluck them, do it gently so you do not damage the skin. Before cooking, wipe the bird inside and out with a dry cloth. You can wash it but be sure to dry it thoroughly afterwards. If you buy pheasants already dressed, or if a nimrod friend gives them to you ready to cook you won't need this good advice. Just cook them and eat them in any of the followings ways. Incidentally, all of these recipes can be used with broiler chickens or Cornish game hen as well as other game birds. Allow 1 bird for 2 people.

ROAST STUFFED PHEASANT

Never, but never, skin pheasant. Rub them well inside
and out with melted butter, salt and pepper and a trace of
ginger. Fill the belly and the craw with your favorite
stuffing, then truss the bird: tie down the wings and legs
close to the body.

Place the birds in a covered roasting pan or baking dish.

Cover them with a clean white cotton cloth which has
been soaked in melted butter or cooking oil. Add two
cups of water, cover, and cook in a 350 degree oven for
one hour, basting every 15 minutes. Remember, the more
you baste, the better the taste! Pour it all over the covering cloth. At the end of the hour, remove the cloth and
brown the bird or birds in a hot oven for 10 minutes.
Remove the trussing strings and place the birds on a platter garnished with baked orange halves covered with
sugar and dotted with red cherries (Bake 15 minutes).
Or, if you want to be really fancy, pour a jigger of brandy
— or better still a jigger of lemon extract — and ignite.
(Lemon extract which is 85% pure grain alcohol [190
proof] is the best flaming agent I know. And it adds
a delightful, mild lemon flavor.)

L. L. BEAN'S ROAST PHEASANT

Many men have reached the status of legends, their achievements and philosophies becoming integral parts of their times and thus lasting influences on future generations. Such was the late L. L. Bean of Freeport, Maine —hunter, fisherman, manufacturer, merchant and philosopher.

He not only hunted and fished throughout the entire State of Maine but travelled far and wide to test his knowledge, skill and equipment in the field, the forest and on inland and coastal waters. Out of his long experience came important inventions and improvements in methods and accoutrements which he developed and offered to the nimrods and Izaak Waltons of the whole country. The L. L. Bean Catalog is not only nationally known and distributed: it is an American classic and a full repository of practical head-to-toe clothing for sportsmen and the most efficient camping, hunting and fishing accessories. Any hunter or fisherman coming to Maine knows the L. L. Bean store, open 24 hours a day, 365 days a year.

His ways of cooking were essentially simple. This is how he roasted pheasant. It's in his own words: "Dress and clean the pheasant. Tie several pieces of fat bacon or salt pork on the breast. Bake 30 to 50 minutes, basting frequently with fat in the pan. Remove bacon or salt pork before serving."

Simple, yes and mighty good!

ROAST PHEASANT IN FOIL

Split pheasants in half down the middle. Allow ½ pheasant per person. Cut out sufficiently large squares of aluminum foil to completely enfold each piece of pheasant.

Place each ½ bird, cut side down, on the piece of foil.

Pour 2 tablespoons of melted butter over each and sprinkle lightly with salt and pepper.

Fold the foil over lightly so that there is a cup in the bottim of each piece. Put 2 tablespoons of light, white wine or beer in the cup and then wrap the foil securely, making it air tight.

Place the birds in an uncovered baking pan and cook at 275 degrees for about 45 minutes. The steam from the wine or beer will tenderize the birds and keep them juicy.

Take out of the oven and place under the broiler for 10 minutes where they will brown through the foil.

To serve, open the foil, place the birds on a platter and pour the remaining juice over them. Garnish with broiled bacon and broiled mushrooms and a sprig or two of greenery such as parsley or watercress.

GRILLED PHEASANT OVER COALS
(WOOD OR CHARCOAL)

Split the pheasant in two as for broiling. For each two pheasants make a sauce of 2 cups of cooking oil, ¾ cup of vinegar, 1 tablespoon salt, 1 teaspoon black pepper, 1 clove of garlic or 1 teaspoon garlic salt and 1 teaspoon of Worcestershire. Marinate them in the sauce overnight.

When ready to cook, pour the sauce into a sauce pan and warm. Place each half pheasant on the grill, taking care to have them far enough from the coals so they will not burn. Cook slowly, basting with the warm sauce every 3 or 4 minutes as you turn the birds from one side to the other. Cooking time is 25 to 35 minutes. Do not overcook.

Serve garnished with greenery and, to enjoy them most, eat them with your fingers. Emily Post and Amy Vanderbilt will have no objections!

PHEASANT PIE À LA 21

This is a specialty of M. Yves Louis Ploneis, chef de cuisine of Jack and Charlie's 21 restaurant in New York.

It is *très magnifique.* For 4 to 6 servings:

6 small onions	*2 tablespoons cooked*
4 quartered mushrooms	*lima beans*
1 quartered carrot	*½ cup roast potato*
2 tablespoons cooked	*parisienne (see*
peas	*page 214)*

1 cup wine (red or white)

Roast two young pheasants as you would a small chicken.

While the birds are cooking, cook the onions, mushrooms, carrot, peas, lima beans and potato. (You can use frozen vegtables.)

Make an unsweetened pie crust.

When the birds are done cut them into small pieces, about 8 to 10 per bird. Remove most of the bones. Put the bones in a deep pot with 2 cupfuls of brown gravy and 1 cup of wine and simmer for ½ hour.

The birds go into a deep baking dish with all the cooked vegetables. Strain the gravy over all. Cover with the pie crust and bake in the oven for ½ hour. Serve hot.

PHEASANT FRICASSEE

Flour	*Olive oil*
4 cups milk	*1 cup cream, sweet*
1 can mushrooms	*or sour*
Salt	*1 small onion or*
Pepper	*3 shallots*
Worcestershire sauce	

If you shoot a couple of tough old cocks, here's a recipe that will do justice to them. One of the tastiest of recipes, it will add to your reputation as a chef!

Wipe the birds with a damp cloth. Cut into serving pieces, dip in flour and fry in olive oil until nicely browned. Add 2 cups of boiling water and let simmer, uncovered, until tender. (The time depends on the size and age.) Add 2 cups of milk, 1 cup of cream and a can of button mushrooms that have been sautéed previously with the finely minced onion or shallots. Stir in 1 tablespoon of flour, mixed with a little water. Season with salt and pepper and a dash of Worcestershire and cook for 15 minutes. Arrange in serving dish, pour over the gravy and mushrooms and sprinkle with 2 tablespoons of chopped parsley. Serve with rice and croutons. 6 generous servings.

PHEASANT À LA WESTMINSTER

For each pheasant you will need:

3 leaves rosemary   *1 teaspoon salt*
¼ leaf thyme   *¼ teaspoon pepper*
1 leaf sage   *2 tablespoons white*
1 tablespoon olive   *wine*
oil   *1 tablespoon sherry*
                    Parsley

Clean pheasant with damp cloth. Chop the herbs very fine and stir them together, then mix with salt, pepper, oil, white wine and sherry. Apply to all parts of the bird, rubbing some inside.

Put 2 pieces of lean salt pork (not bacon) over the breast. Place in a roasting pan with a carrot and a sprig of celery.

Roast at 350 degrees for 30 to 35 minutes. After the bird starts to brown, puncture the breast with a long fork and baste every ten minutes while roasting for another 40 minutes. (Remember: the more you baste, the better the taste.)

PHEASANT À LA MARYLAND

Quarter or disjoint pheasant just as you would a chicken for frying. Wet each piece and dip in flour seasoned with salt and pepper and ground rosemary.

Pre-heat a sufficient amount of cooking oil in a large skillet and pan fry the pieces, uncovered, until they are golden brown. At this point add a cup or two of water and simmer slowly until tender. This should take about 20 minutes and the water should have simmered down to a thick, golden gravy. Garnish the serving platter with pineapple slices, red cherries and greenery. Serves 3 or 4.

PHEASANT IN WINE

Quarter or cut into serving pieces. Dice 4 ounces of fat bacon and fry quickly in an earthenware casserole in a little butter with six small onions. Be sure not to burn.

When the onions are golden, add the pheasant pieces, a few mushrooms, a sprig of thyme, a bay leaf and some parsley. Cook, covered, over a brisk fire. Skim occasionally. When the pheasant is done, remove from dish and keep warm. Add a half pint of vintage red wine and salt and pepper to the sauce. Thicken with a little butter and flour. Remove the herbs and pour over the meat.

Garnish with croutons and triangular slices of lemon.

Serves 4.

BREAST OF PHEASANT WITH RICE
(WILD OR HERBED)

Breasts of 3 or 4 large	*1 teaspoon grated*
pheasants (skinned)	*onion*
½ cup butter	*2 cups heavy cream*
1 pound mushrooms,	*4 teaspoons brandy*
sliced	*4 teaspoons dry*
½ teaspoon salt	*sherry*

Wild or Herbed Rice
(Herb regular cooked rice with herbs of your choice)

Wipe the breasts, season with salt and pepper. Sauté in butter over low heat for 20 minutes or until a rich brown.

Remove and keep hot.

Add mushrooms and onion to the butter remaining in the pan and cook for 5 minutes, stirring constantly. Reduce the heat, add the cream and continue stirring. Simmer for 5 minutes, then add the brandy and sherry and simmer 5 minutes longer.

Arrange the pheasant on rice and pour over the hot sauce. 6 to 8 servings.

PHEASANT BREASTS WITH HAM

This is a very fine way of using left over roast pheasant, if you ever have any. It will serve 6.

7 slices pheasant	*1 box or can of mush-*
breast	*rooms*
7 slices ham	*1 teaspoon paprika*
½ onion, chopped	*1 teaspoon salt*
¼ pound butter	*1 teaspoon nutmeg*
¾ cup sweet cream	*Grated Parmesan*
	cheese

Cook the onion in butter until soft, not brown, add the mushrooms, cut in half, and the seasonings and simmer for 15 minutes.

Turn into an ovenproof dish (from which you will serve), arrange the meat on top of the mushrooms. Add hot (but not boiling) cream. Sprinkle with grated Parmesan cheese and place in a 400 degree oven for 10 minutes. Serve immediately.

BRAISED PHEASANT, SWEET AND SOUR

1 cup water
1 cup white, seedless
  raisins
½ cup pitted red sour
  or sweet cherries
½ cup canned pine-
  apple, cut into
  small chunks

2 tablespoons sugar
2 tablespoons vinegar
¼ teaspoon sour salt
  (citric acid) if you
  have it. If not, skip
  it. A light shake
  of curry powder.

Simmer all of the above for five minutes in a sauce pan.

The pheasants are to be split down the middle (½ bird per person). Place the halves in a large skillet in cooking oil or butter. Brown on each side. When browned turn down the heat. Pour the sauce over the birds and simmer slowly for 15 minutes, then salt to taste.

When serving pour the fruited sauce over the pheasants and garnish with greenery. I assure you this is as delicious as it is different.

PHEASANT MOLLE

(PHEASANT WITH CHOCOLATE SAUCE)

This may sound not so good but it is truly a delightful and exotic dish. Two pheasants should serve 4 to 6 persons, depending, of course, on the heartiness of their appetites.

Quarter each pheasant so that you have the drum stick and thigh and part of the backs in two sections. Halve the breast each with a wing and the rest of the back. Place in a baking pan and add 7 cups lightly salted water. Simmer, covered, in a 275 degree oven for about 1½ hours. Remove from oven. Cover pheasant with melted butter and brown under the broiler until just a light brown. Keep warm.

MOLLE SAUCE

There are a number of variations. If you don't want to go to the trouble of making it yourself, it can be bought at specialty food shops. Anyway here's my recipe for making it. It's worth a try.

2 cloves garlic	*2 teaspoons anise seed*
2 onions	*¾ cup red chili*
Butter	*powder*
6 cups bouillon	*1 teaspoon black*
6 squares bitter	*pepper*
chocolate	*1 cup peanut butter*
1 teaspoon oregano	*½ cup corn meal*
leaves	*Salt*

2 teaspoons ground cinnamon

Chop up the 2 cloves of garlic and the 2 onions and simmer gently in a skillet in ¼ pound stick of butter. Add 6 cups of bouillon, 6 squares of bitter chocolate, 2 teaspoons ground cinnamon, ¾ cup of red chili powder, 2 teaspoons anise seed, 1 teaspoon oregano leaves and 1 teaspoon black pepper. Simmer gently, stirring constantly. When the chocolate is all melted, add 1 cup of peanut butter and thicken with ½ cup of corn meal. Salt to taste. Keep stirring. When thoroughly mixed, place the pheasant back in the roasting pan, pour over the sauce and cook in a 275 degree oven for 10 minutes. Serve bubbling hot.

If you wish, cut up toasted almonds or toasted sesame seeds and add to the sauce. If a really hot sauce is desired, add red hot pepper sauce or a level teaspoon of ground red pepper.

PARTRIDGE (GROUSE*) AND QUAIL

Partridge, like pheasant, are fine and noble game birds. They offer the hunter great sport and the cook great opportunities to produce gastronomic sensations. Young partridge, especially, is much to be desired. Yet the birds should not be too young: they must be mature enough for the meat to have developed its delicate, specific flavor. You can tell young from old by the color of their legs: yellow in the young; gray or gray-black in the older bird. Also the young have two very pointed outside "wing feathers"; in the old they are rounded.

(*The asterisk above is to tell you, if you don't already know, that partridge and grouse are one and the same in North America. In some regions they are called by one name; in others — and even in the same region — the other.)

I wish it were possible for you to enjoy Hungarian Partridge. Called The Hun by the upland game cognoscenti, it is
a very sporty bird, full breasted and with darker, more tender and more succulent meat than our American birds. It is
rated by many as the greatest upland delicacy. Cooking methods are the same as for pheasant, partridge or quail.

Quail, a member of the partridge family, fly and live
like The Huns but are only a half or a quarter their size. They
must be eaten soon after shooting. The meat is dry and without special flavor, therefore, season well to help it along.

Young partridges should roast 35 to 40 minutes — the
meat should be still pink near the bone. The use of strong
spices is definitely out. Bacon, sour or sweet cream, fresh
herbs and red wine are good complements.

ROAST PARTRIDGE OR RUFFED GROUSE

I like partridge best just plain roasted and served with
the sauce of the butter in which it was cooked. Salt and
pepper inside and out. Preheat oven to 450 degrees. Lard
the breasts and place the birds in an open pan. Roast 15
minutes on each side and 15 minutes on the back — in all
45 minutes. Baste every 10 to 15 minutes with melted
butter. Allow a whole partridge for hearty eaters, half
for others. Garnish with lemons, quartered, and sprinkle with paprika and lots of watercress, arranged in
tufts. 1 bird serves 1 or 2.

ROAST STUFFED PARTRIDGE

Soak the bird overnight in water to which has been added 1 tablespoon of baking soda. Next day dry thoroughly. Make your favorite stuffing and stuff as you would a pheasant (see page 94). Wrap strips of bacon around the bird. Take a sheet of aluminum foil large enough to wrap it completely. Grease the inside of the paper with Crisco. Place the birds on greased side, wrap tightly. Put in 350 degree oven. A small bird will take about an hour; a larger one an hour and a half. Serve with bread sauce (see page 199 and red currant jelly. 1 bird serves 2.

PARTRIDGE ST. SAUVEUR

4 young partridge or ptarmigan
4 slices bacon
2 to 3 tablespoons butter
1 small onion
½ cup sweet cream

Dry the birds inside and out. Rub with salt and pepper and wrap in bacon. If you have a grape leaf put it under the bacon: it will give the meat a lovely flavor and keep the breasts moist. Put inside each a piece of butter, some grapes and elderberries. (The elderberries are favorite partridge food. If you have none, rub the birds sparingly with gin.)

Place in a casserole and pour over hot melted butter. Add minced onion and roast in a 400 degree oven for about 30 minutes. At the last minute pour on the cream. Serve with mashed potatoes and sauerkraut cooked in champagne and pineapple (see page 210), or with a chicory salad mixed with pineapple. Serves 4.

ROAST GROUSE IN SOUR CREAM

Cut up one or more birds into serving pieces, 1 for 2 servings. Roll in flour seasoned with 1 teaspoon of finely crushed dry or fresh tarragon. Brown in frying fat in a skillet then place in a roasting pan, dabbing 1 teaspoon of sour cream on each piece. Cover and bake for 1 hour at 375 degrees. Baste once with sour cream during cooking. Make gravy by adding sour cream and thinning with liquid from a can of mushrooms. Add the mushrooms.

Pour over the meat on the platter and garnish with red currant jelly or spiced currants. Serve with wild rice.

This recipe may also be used for pheasant or young chicken. Don't tell anybody but to make partridge or pheasant go farther, you can add a broiler or two, cut into small pieces. The chicken will absorb something of the flavor of the game and will stand you in good stead when there's a call for seconds or thirds!

PARTRIDGE POLONAISE

A favorite of Dorothea Countess Michelska. Salt partridge and wrap in bacon. Roast, uncovered in a 375 degree oven about 35 minutes or until light brown. Sprinkle with paprika, add enough sweet cream to half cover the bird then add fresh mushrooms and cook until they are soft. Serve with mashed potatoes.

VELOUTÉ OF PARTRIDGE À LA ELISABETH, PRINCESS ALTENBURG

This is a particularly good way to prepare young, badly shot birds. Roast two or three partridge in butter at 350 degrees for no more than 20 minutes. Remove the breast meat and reserve. Put the legs and bones back into the pan and roast for another 15 minutes. Add 1 tablespoon of brandy and 2 cups of chicken consommé and simmer for 15 minutes. Then put through a sieve and add one cup of light cream and 1 beaten egg yolk. Do not allow it to boil. Cut the breast meat into fine strips and add. 6 servings.

PARTRIDGE FLAMBÉE

2 partridge	*Elderberries or*
5 tablespoons liver	*grapes*
paté	*Salt*
3 tablespoons butter	*Pepper*
Pinch of thyme	*8 tablespoons brandy*

For this the partridge should be hung for 3 days. When ready sauté them in butter for 20 minutes over a hot flame. Carefully remove the meat from the bones: each bird should be in four pieces — 2 breasts and 2 legs. Take all bones — the whole carcass including the head and press through a heavy juice-press. Squeeze all juices from the bones. Chop finely the hearts, liver and gizzards and add them to the juices together with the liver paté.

Place the meat in a chafing dish and pour the juice over. Mix well over medium heat. Add some butter, thyme, elderberries or grapes (the grapes cut fine), salt and pepper to taste. Cook for two minutes, then stir in the brandy. Set it aflame and continue stirring gently until the flames have died. Serve immediately on toast spread with butter and covered with liver paté. 4 to 6 servings.

PARTRIDGE EN GELÉE (WITH TRUFFLES)

I particularly like this regal dish. It is truly fit for a king or a banker you want to impress! And it is prepared the day before.

Lard the partridge with thin slices of truffles. Use a larding needle to draw them through the gashes you have made in the breasts. Insert them about an inch apart, at right angles to the breast bone. Roast in butter, wine and chopped parsley for 30 minutes. (At 350 degrees). Set them aside to cool.

When cool, carefully cut the breast meat from the bones. You want whole half breasts. Rinse a casserole or Pyrex dish with cold water. Fill the bottom with consommé to which gelatin has been added. Put in strips of truffles and ham and let it set. Then put in the breasts and more gelatine and consommé. Refrigerate overnight. Turn out of the dish onto a platter and garnish with greenery. Serve with mayonnaise.

SHERRY BAKED PTARMIGAN

Ptarmigan are a species of grouse found in northern areas. They are distinguished by completely feathered feet. Of course, pheasant or partridge may be substituted.

2 *Ptarmigan, cut up*	2 *pints whipping or*
6 *tablespoons butter*	*table cream*
or bacon fat	*Salt*
½ *cup sherry*	*Pepper*

Use a flame proof casserole to sauté the ptarmigan in the butter or bacon fat. In about 10 minutes it will be golden brown on all sides. Pour off almost all of the drippings.

Add the cream, sherry and salt and pepper. Cover the casserole with aluminum foil then with the casserole lid to make as airtight as possible. Bake at 350 degrees until the ptarmigan is tender — about 35 to 45 minutes. Serves 2.

BREAST OF PARTRIDGE ON CHESTNUT PURÉE

Finely chop the liver and other parts of the bird except the breast. Make a fine paste and spread on the breasts which have been cut from the bone. Sauté in butter for 10 minutes. Then roll the meat in flour and roast in a 350 degree oven for another 20 minutes. Arrange on the chestnut purée (see page 212) and serve with brown sauce to which is added 3 tablespoons of Madeira wine.

QUAIL MORENCY

(à la Mary von Motzeck, Dogwood Plantation, Estill, South Carolina)

Split quail up the back and break to lie it flat. You'll need 2 quail per person. Brown both sides in butter on top of the stove in a heavy iron skillet. Change to a casserole.

Add 1 tablespoon of tart apple or currant jelly, one or two ounces of sherry or white wine and one tablespoon of orange peel per quail. (Peel the orange and scrape clean.

Using a grapefruit knife, scrape the inside of the peel until it is almost paper thin. Then cut it into strips twice the width of a kitchen match and about as long.)

Cover the casserole and simmer for 30 minutes. Serve on dark, buttered toast with the sauce on the side.

RAGOUT OF QUAIL

(Another fine recipe from Elisabeth, Princess Altenburg)

Cut quail in half. Roll in flour and brown on both sides in bacon fat. Add ½ cup of consommé or a bouillon cube dissolved in water. Make a bouquet garni of 2 sprigs of parsley, 1 piece of celery, thyme, bay leaf and, if you wish, a leek, a pinch of marjoram and a leaf of tarragon. Add sliced mushrooms and/or artichoke bottoms (optional). Salt and pepper.

Cook slowly at 350 degrees for 30 minutes and add the juice of 1 orange. 1½ quail per serving is generous.

QUAIL PIE À LA PIGNON ROUGE

Pignon Rouge is the name of our house at St. Sauveur in the Laurentians. It seems appropriate to thus name this dish, for it was created there to make the most of badly shot birds which we had shot and frozen in South Carolina.

8 quail	*Flour*
Butter	*Salt and pepper*
1 onion, minced	*Cornstarch*
8 tablespoons celery,	*3 tablespoons cognac*
minced	*1 can mushrooms*

Cut all meat from the bones and roll in flour seasoned with salt and pepper. Brown in butter until golden brown 1 medium minced onion and 8 tablespoons minced celery (no leaves). Then add 1 can or ½ pound of mushrooms.

Brown the floured quail in another pan. Put in 1 can of chicken broth, a tablespoon of cornstarch for thickening and the cognac. Seal with an appropriately sized pie crust. (Cut vents to allow steam to escape.) Bake at 350 degrees until the crust is nice and brown. Serves 6.

Optional: Serve with small pancakes made of pie crust.

QUAIL PIE, SOUTH CAROLINA

6 quail	*1 cup diced celery*
4 tablespoons butter	*4 cups chicken broth*
2 tablespoons cooking oil	*2 cups diced cooked ham*
1 can sliced mushrooms	*Flour*
1 medium onion, minced	*Salt and pepper*

Cut the quail into serving pieces. (I use either shot-up or unhurt quail, taking the raw meat off the bones.)

Coat with flour, seasoned with salt and pepper. Brown on all sides in butter and cooking oil. (The latter keeps it from burning.) Remove the quail. In the same pan sauté the onion and mushrooms for 5 minutes. Return the quail to the skillet and add the celery, chicken broth and salt and pepper. Cover and simmer for 10 minutes.

Now place the quail and ham in a 3 quart casserole. Mix 1½ tablespoons of flour or cornstarch with 3 tablespoons of water, stir into the mixture in the skillet and cook until thickened. Pour over the meat in the casserole and add a liqueur glass of cognac.

Fit the pie crust over the casserole and cut vents to allow the steam to escape. Bake at 350 degrees for 40 to 50 minutes or until the crust is brown. 4 servings.

WOODCOCK AND SNIPE

Woodcock should be prepared like partridge. When shot during the winter woodcock are small and skinny while the fall birds are plump and fat — and more tender. Hang the birds in "feather dress" for a few days. In the old days woodcock were roasted without removing the entrails but our tastes have changed and the entrails are removed — and often used to make very special appetizers.

The snipe is one of the aristocrats of upland game. Belonging to the same family as woodcock, they are small and very like quail with a beak about two inches long. They are a great delicacy when shot at their fattest in the fall. Pluck the birds carefully up to the neck, then pull the skin over the head and remove the eyes with small sharp knife. Singe their long legs over a flame, remove the skin and stretch the legs backward, tying them to a little piece of wood or just with string. Take out the stomach, windpipe and crop. Other entrails may be left inside if you wish. As with other birds, badly shot snipe — or very skinny ones — should be used only in stews, pies, soups or patés. The following recipes can be used for either woodcock or snipe.

WOODCOCK ENTRAILS APPETIZERS

All entrails are taken out (heart, liver, guts but throw away the stomach.) Chop all finely and mix with a little bacon, minced onion, parsley and cook with salt and a small glass of red wine. Combine butter with bread crumbs and season with marjoram and basil. It should have the consistency of a thick paste.

Arrange on small buttered white bread squares, sprinkle with butter and/or grated parmesan cheese and place in the oven for 5 to 6 minutes.

WOODCOCK HORS D'OEUVRES

Use badly shot birds for these. Chop finely the wood-cock meats and entrails, some shallots and parsley and sauté in butter. Then mix with 1 tablespoon of flour, 1 beaten egg yolk, and 1 tablespoon of Madeira wine or Harvey's Shooting Sherry.

Toast buttered white bread. Cut off the crusts. Spread the paste on the toast and bake in a 350 degree oven for 10 minutes.

WOODCOCK À LA SIMPSON

This was a favorite with Sir George Simpson, Governor of the Hudson Bay, circa 1821. Clean the bird and dry inside and out. Rub with salt and pepper and wrap in bacon.

Cut a thick slice of white bread. Remove the crusts and shape into a rectangle. Toast in butter on one side only then cover the untoasted side with a generous amount of liver paté. Place the bird on it and put it into a buttered roasting pan in a 375 degree oven for 20 minutes.

Now comes the important — and obligatory part. When the bird is done, heat one tablespoon of brandy, light it and pour over the bird. Serve while still flaming.

TIMBERDOODLE PIE WITH MUSHROOMS

Red Wine
Saffron
1 tablespoon mono-
    sodium glutinate
    or wild game sea-
    soning

Flour
Arrowroot or Corn-
    starch
1 cup canned or fresh
    chopped mushroom
    caps

Salt and pepper

For 6 persons take at least 6 badly shot woodcock (timberdoodles) and simmer in water until tender — approximately an hour. Season the water with saffron which will give the gravy a nice yellow color.

Strain the broth into another pan, adding 2 pats of butter. Pick the meat off the birds and put into the broth.

Thicken with flour, arrowroot or cornstarch. Add salt and pepper, 1 tablespoon of monosodium glutinate or wild game seasoning and 1 cup of canned or fresh chopped mushroom caps. Pour in ½ cup or more of red wine according to the number of birds.

Grease your most suitable casserole with butter and line the bottom with a thick, short pie crust. Fill casserole with the thickened meat and gravy and top with another crust. Crimp the edges of the crust with a fork, cut vents to let out the steam and brush with beaten egg. Place in a 350 degree oven and bake until golden brown. Note: The wine is a *must*. And in making the crust don't be stingy with the shortening. Make it really short!

This same recipe is excellent with snipe, quail, pheasant, dove or rabbit.

ROAST SNIPE (OR WOODCOCK)

8 birds	*6 tablespoons butter*
4 slices bacon	*1 onion minced*

Salt and pepper

Clean the birds and wipe them dry. Rub inside and out
with salt and pepper and wrap in bacon. Put the butter
in the roasting pan and when hot add the birds and
minced onion and roast for 20 minutes in a 350 degree
oven. Garnish with croutons and lemon slices. 5 servings.

ROAST SNIPE IN FOIL

1 egg	*Tarragon*
Bread crumbs	*Olive Oil*
Butter	*Grapes*
Rosemary	*Parsley*

Salt and pepper

Brush each snipe with beaten egg yolk and roll in bread
crumbs. Place a lump of butter on each bird and roast
12 to 15 minutes in a 350 degree oven. Season while cooking with salt and pepper, a little rosemary or tarragon
(USE SPARINGLY).

Or, if you prefer, season each bird first with salt and pepper, rub with olive oil and put some grapes and parsley
in the cavities. Wrap in greased foil and roast in 350
degree oven for 20 minutes. Allow 1 or 2 snipe per
person.

SOUTHERN FRIED SNIPE

Sear small pin feathers, if necessary. Wet the birds and dip them in flour seasoned with salt and pepper. A little ground rosemary, thyme or wild game seasoning is good added to the flour. The easiest way to coat the birds (you probably know this) is to put the seasoned flour into a paper bag, shake, then put the birds in and shake again for a minute.

Preheat enough cooking oil in a large skillet to cover the birds. Deep fry until they are golden brown. Drain and place on toast. Serve with wild rice and cranberry jelly, fiddleheads or artichoke hearts. 1 or 2 snipe per person.

SNIPE WITH PATÉ

Split snipe down the back, rub with butter and broil 10 to 12 minutes. Season with salt and pepper and serve on toast spread with paté. 1 or 2 snipe per serving.

You can use a can of chicken liver paté, a very fine calves' liverwurst or, if you want to be extravagant and go whole hog, paté de fois gras from Strasbourg.

SNIPE OR WOODCOCK CROUTONS

These are really great appetizers.

Entrails of 8 snipe	*½ tablespoon minced*
or woodcock	*parsley*
2 to 3 tablespoons	*2 teaspoons lemon*
butter	*juice*
2 tablespoons flour	*2 tablespoons red*
4 egg yolks, beaten	*wine*
4 slices bacon	*2 teaspoons brandy*
2 minced shallots	*Slices of white bread*

Salt and pepper

Finely mince the entrails (except the stomachs) with the bacon. Simmer a few minutes in butter. Add all other ingredients and simmer until thickened. Strain through a sieve. You should have a good thick paste.

Cut white bread into 1½ or 2 inch squares or triangles and cover with the paste — not too thinly. Put into a 400 degree oven for a few minutes shortly before serving.

BIRDS MISCELLANEOUS

ROAST WILD TURKEY

Wild Turkey tends to be very dry unless cooked carefully. Rub inside and out with melted butter, then ground ginger. Stuff the cavity and craw opening loosely with your favorite dressing. (Use lots of butter in the dressing but keep it reasonably dry.) Sew the skin over the craw and the bottom cavity. Tie the legs firmly and cut off any extra string. Salt and pepper the outside.

Now melt more butter and soak a clean, white cotton cloth in it and wrap around the bird. Place breast side up on a wire rack in a large roasting pan with cover. Pour about 4 cups of water into the bottom. Cover and roast in 300 to 325 degree oven. The time for cooking, of course, depends on the size of the bird. Allow 20 minutes per pound. Baste with liquid in the pan, re-saturating the cotton cloth frequently. Test for tenderness by sticking a fork into the thick part of the thigh. If it turns easily, the bird is done.

To finish the job, remove the cloth covering and brown quickly in a hot oven in the uncovered pan.

Wild turkey gizzards are tough and the liver strong. If you have a yen for them, simmer in water for a long time but I recommend not putting them in the gravy.

DOVE À LA MARY VON MOTZECK

The wild pigeon is a particularly succulent and flavor-full morsel. This recipe is another creation of my friend from South Carolina.

Stuff each dove with 1 tablespoon of canned mincemeat, salt and pepper to taste. Wrap with a slice of bacon. Place in a shallow, covered baking pan. Mix 1 table-spoon of sherry and 1 tablespoon of apple jelly for each dove and put over the bird. (Make a little extra for basting.) Bake at 350 degrees for 40 minutes. Allow 1 or 2 birds per person.

RAMEREAUX OLIVES (PIGEONS WITH OLIVES)

A favorite dish of Toulouse Lautrec, it is a true culinary masterpiece!

Stuff young pigeons with beef, veal and sausage meat, spiced with aromatic pepper, nutmeg and sliced truffles. Tie them with string and fry lightly in butter in a stew pan. Meanwhile, put butter, diced bacon, shallots or onions in a casserole. Make a white sauce with flour and add with salt and pepper, parsley and a pinch of thyme and marjoram. Put the pigeons in and cover with good stock or consomme. Simmer gently, covered, for an hour. During the last 20 minutes add green, well-soaked, stoned olives and a glass of brandy. Braise and reduce heat.

Arrange pigeons in a serving dish, surround them with the olives and cover with the strained sauce. (It should be fairly thick.) 1 bird per serving.

DOVES OR PIGEONS IN JELLY

This chef d'oeuvre was given me by one of the most famous Greek chefs, Constantinos Kapreli, who created it for the great hunter, Hans von Aulock. It was when Kapreli was on the Bosporus where princes, high aristocracy and diplomats enjoyed his great cuisine.

It calls for 10 doves (or tourterelle, woodcock, quail, partridge or duck). Place them in a casserole with cooking fat, salt, pepper, 1 carrot, 1 stalk of celery, 1 onion and one apple and roast until done. Remove the breasts and set aside.

In a large mold pour a layer (about 1 inch deep) of consommé to which gelatin has been added. (Approximately 4 cups of consommé to one envelope gelatin.) Garnish with sliced truffles, capers and sliced cornichons (gherkins). Chill until firm. Now place the breasts on the jell and pour over more consommé and gelatin until the birds are covered. Chill until firm. Unmold before serving. 1 or 2 birds per person.

DOVES PRAISE ALLAH

8 to 12 doves	*Salt and black pepper*
2 tablespoons cooking oil	*1½ cups water*
2 hefty pats of butter	*Praise Allah seasoning*

In a skillet place 2 tablespoons of cooking oil and 2 pats of butter. Brown the doves on both sides at 350 degrees (medium heat). When brown add 1½ cups of water, a good shake each of salt and black pepper and several shakes of Praise Allah seasoning (see page 132).

Allow the doves to simmer at low heat, tightly covered, for 45 minutes, turning them only once, and adding a touch of water if needed. All water should cook away before serving.

Asparagus, green peas, buttered lima beans or green beans, plus brown or wild rice and a tossed green salad are good dishes to go with a dove dinner.

DOVES BASCOM

8 to 12 doves	*5 large pats of butter*
1 cup red wine	*½ teaspoon salt*
½ teaspoon black pepper	*12 dried juniper berries or 1 teaspoon gin*

Marinate the doves overnight in a good red wine. Pepper well. When ready to prepare them for the table, wipe doves dry and brown them in butter in a skillet. Remove to a roasting pan, with cover, pour the butter remaining in the skillet over them, add the marinating wine, salt and the juniper berries or gin.

Cook in a 350 degree oven for 45 minutes, basting them two or three times. Let all liquid cook off before serving.

PRAIRIE CHICKEN

Use a good pheasant or quail recipe. Or stuff them with wild rice and bake — wonderful way to cook them.

CROWS

Young crows are very tasty although many people have an aversion to eating crow. They are generally fat and the taste is much like pigeon — and they can be prepared like them. Don't hang them too long, however, and don't pluck but skin them. As the skin is dark it is not very appetizing looking. Brown the birds well and serve as you would partridge.

HOT CROW'S NEST

An unusual, delectable way of preparing and serving crows and reasonably easy to put together.

Cut into small pieces all the meat except the breasts of 2 or 3 roasted crows. (Leave breasts whole.) To the cut up meat add a large teaspoon of anchovy paste and 3 tablespoons of finely chopped parsley, 1 tablespoon finely chopped chives, ⅓ teaspoon tarragon leaves, a small can of small shrimps, 2 tablespoons of mayonnaise or white sauce, salt and monosodium glutinate.

Slice evenly thick bread squares and roast in butter until light brown. Arrange the above mixture, piled high, on the bread, place the breasts on top and put in the oven to heat through. 1 crow per serving. Serve with green salad.

ROAST FIELD LARKS

It is against the law in many parts of North America to kill field larks even though they are very plentiful and afford good jump shooting. The law permitting, here's an excellent way to prepare them. You'll want 2 or 3 per person.

Pick feathers, cut off feet and head, split down the back and clean thoroughly. Lay them breast up in a roasting pan and cover each breast with a piece of bacon. Pepper lightly with black pepper. Roast in a 350 degree oven for 20 minutes. Remove and sprinkle bread crumbs over tops. Baste with the juices in the pan and put back in a slower oven (300 degrees) for about five minutes. Serve piping hot.

LIVER OF FEATHERED GAME

Prepare just as you do chicken livers: wash and remove the gall (in some birds there is none). Cook two minutes on each side in fat and onion rings. Only salt afterwards. If you have any left over gravy or some sour cream, pour this into the pan, seasoned with "Praise Allah,"* vinegar and a little sugar. Serve in individual dishes or use as filling for omelets.

---

*A gourmet's delight from the Old Thyme Spice House, Davis Manufacturing Co., Knoxville, Tennessee, and available in all good stores, it is a wonderful seasoning for steaks, meats, stews and gravies.

FINNED GAME

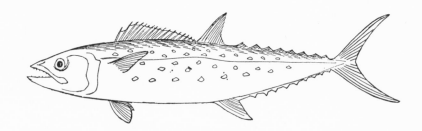

Through the ages the virtues of fish and the arts of catching and cooking them have been more than adequately recorded by literary greats, accomplished anglers, philosophers, Baron Munchhausens, master chefs and grateful housewives. Not the least of these was Aristotle, that man of many talents. As were most Ancient Greeks, he was extremely fond of fish and even wrote a "cook book" describing the different species in Aegean waters and making suggestions on cooking and seasoning them. "Best of all," he wrote, "I like the widowed Amia, a fine and dainty fish, wrapped in fig leaves, soaked through with oil and, over all with swaddling clothes of marjoram, did I fold it and hid it like a torch beneath the ashes."

Of course, when one speaks of fish and fishing the name Izaak Walton comes immediately to mind. According to the Encyclopedia Britannica, "There is hardly a name in English literature, even of the first rank, whose immortality is more secure, or whose personality is the subject of a more enthusiastic cult. Walton hooked a much bigger fish than he angled for when, in 1653, he offered his quaint treatise THE COMPLEAT ANGLER to the public. His original discourses were added to and refined during the next quarter century. And the additions were not merely technical: happy quotations, new turns of phrase, songs, poems and anecdotes were introduced as if the leisurely author, who wrote it as a recreation, had kept it constantly in his mind and talked it over point by point with his numerous brethren."

The written and verbal lore about fish and fishing is extensive. Methods of angling are as diverse as the individuals who cast, troll, handline, set trawl, harpoon or seine for them. The exaggerated, but nevertheless amusing, stories having to do with size and quantity of the catch are legion. And, as for preparing them for the table, there are a myriad recipes, from simple boiling to the most elaborate culinary creations.

While I admit to being an ardent angler, I have no intention in these pages of expounding on the many theories and techniques of angling. This is, after all, a book designed to help you prepare and serve all kinds of game, a collection of recipes and instructions which have appealed to me and may offer a few new cooking wrinkles that will appeal to you.

Thus, with fish as with other game, I list herein basic cooking methods together with a considerable number of exciting dishes that I have enjoyed over the years.

A FEW COOKING HINTS

Fish cooked in a 450 degree oven require 10 minutes per inch of thickness.

Fish cooked in a 350 degree oven require 20 minutes per inch of thickness. If you use a cream, egg or cheese sauce NEVER cook fish in an oven higher than 350 degrees, as the sauce will separate.

To boil fish: wrap it in cheesecloth, or if this is not available, find a flat rock, put it in the bottom of the pot and place the fish on it. Pour boiling water over and bring it back to boil then turn the heat off and let it stand for 10 minutes for trout and small fish, but for salmon and large fish boil or steam 10 minutes to the pound.

Time to fry or broil fish depends on the size as well as any coating you may use. A flour coating, for example, will take less time than bread crumbs. In any case, cook until golden brown. Test with a fork: it should flake easily.

As to a batter for deep fried fish, see deep fried snipe (page 124).

When fish is cooked from the frozen state the time for cooking must be doubled.

STEAMED FISH

Hang a sieve over the water. Salt the fish and place it in sieve. Cover.

FISH STEAMED IN FOIL

A very good way for any type of fish. Just wrap in foil after adding salt and spices and place in a 350 degree oven.

FRIED FISH

Very dry fish are best fried. Cut large fish into fillets or 1 inch thick cotelettes (cutlets or steaks). Small fish should be whole. Season with salt, a little curry or pepper, paprika or nutmeg. Roll in flour, egg and breadcrumbs or in flour alone. The oil, or better yet butter, should be smoking hot. Use a generous amount of fat: the fish must almost swim in it so it will not stick to the pan.

BAKED FISH

Season with salt, pepper or curry, nutmeg or paprika. Sprinkle with lemon juice, roll in flour and then in lightly beaten egg white. Cover with breadcrumbs, place in smoking hot fat and bake in 425 degree oven to a golden brown.

GRILLED FISH

As mentioned above big fish should be filleted or sliced into cutlets or steaks. Small ones should be grilled whole.

Clean as usual. Do not salt, so that the juice stays in. Brush with melted butter or oil and place on well heated grill. Turn the fish twice on each side. When done put on a platter, season with salt, a little paprika or curry, dust with a little dry mustard and sprinkle with lemon juice.

Garnish with lemon slices and parsley.

FISH AU GRATIN

Place cleaned and seasoned fish in a Pyrex dish that has been well greased. Cover with cheese and pour over hot oil or melted butter to moisten the cheese well. Bake in 350 degree oven until golden brown.

BOILED FISH (BLUE*)

Excellent for delicate fish like trout, salmon, but also for eel and pike and other less sportive fish.

Do not spoil the special flavor of these fish with too much spice. Use just a little salt, a little white wine or vinegar*, a slice of lemon, some carrots and a few slices of onion.

There has to be enough water to almost cover. Place fish in simmering water, let it come to a boil and remove from heat—do not boil hard. Let it stand. 8 to 10 minutes is sufficient for small trout. When the eyes protrude and the fins come off easily, it is done. A very large salmon may be simmered — VERY SLOWLY.
Remember, fish dries very easily and the skin breaks which make it look very unappetizing.

If you want to serve a large fish whole and standing with

*Blue: so called because the white wine or vinegar brings back the color of the fish.

its back up, put 2 big sticks of raw potato inside the belly. Smaller fish are served lying on their side. If you wish you can serve small trout biting its tail: make a big hole behind the head and pull the tail through.

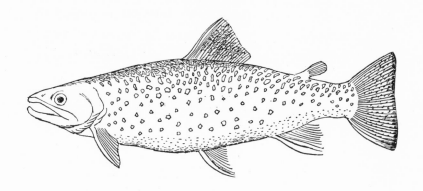

MOUNTAIN, BROOK, RAINBOW, GOLDEN TROUT

If you have caught any of these wonderful game fish I don't need to tell you that they should be cleaned as soon as possible, leaving the heads and tails on. And, before heading for home, look for some young ferns. Cover the bottom of the creel with fern, place a couple of sprigs in the cavity of each, then cover all with more fern. When cooked you will find that the fern has enhanced their flavor and you will enjoy the sweetest morsels you have ever tasted! Also young ferns keep them fresher.

A whole cook book could be written on the cooking of trout, as any French chef might tell you. I am giving you only a few methods. You can carry on from these because most fancy names put on trout dishes are merely variants of the basic ways of garnishing, saucing or serving below.

TRUITE BLEUE (BLUE TROUT)

4 bouillon cubes   *2 pinches dried thyme*
1 quart water   *Tips of 1 stalk of celery*
1 bay leaf   *4 or 5 peppercorns*
1 tablespoon minced   *(or 5 to 6 turns on*
  onion   *your pepper mill)*
1 or 2 sprigs parsley   *¾ cup white wine*

Make a court bouillon, in a skillet, of the bouillon cubes and water to which has been added all of the above ingredients but the wine. Simmer gently for 5 minutes. Leave on the stove, turn up the heat and add the wine. In the meantime you should have the fresh, cleaned trout ready on a platter. Boil ½ cup of white vinegar and pour over the fish. (This will bring out the color of the fish and make the skin come off easily.) Discard the vinegar.

When the court bouillon has come to a boil, place the trout in it. It takes only a few minutes to fully cook. Drain and serve immediately with salted lemon butter (lemon juice and butter) poured over the trout. Or serve the sauce separately.

Use the same recipe for small salmon — 8 to 15 inches. 4 trout — 4 servings.

BAKED STUFFED TROUT OR SALMON

Larger trout and fresh water or landlocked salmon from 3 to 6 pounds in weight are easier to handle if stuffed and baked. They may be baked unstuffed but the stuffing will absorb a lot of the good juices of the fish that you would otherwise lose.

Let's leave the skin, head and tail on our choice finned friend. Clean out the cavity and fill with your favorite stuffing: bread and celery, bread and oysters, bread and crab meat, mushrooms and wild rice or whatever you choose.

Now close the abdomen with coarse thread or metal clamps. (Remove after cooking and before serving.)

Place your masterpiece in an oven pan which has been well greased to prevent sticking. Pour melted butter over the fish and put 3 or 4 strips of bacon on the top. Salt and pepper and further season with savory sea food seasoning or monosodium glutinate (3 or 4 energetic shakes — optional) and sprinkle on paprika.

Bake, uncovered, about 12 minutes for each pound in a 375 degree oven. Baste several times with the juices, remembering the old rule — "the more you baste, the better the taste." 6 to 8 servings.

PAN FRIED TROUT

Do not attempt to scale the fish and do not remove the head, tail or skin. Rinse and dip from head to tail in whole wheat flour (white cornmeal may be used instead). Season with salt and pepper.

Place the trout in a pre-heated skillet with sufficient cooking oil (or butter), and fry at about 350 degrees (medium heat) until golden brown on both sides. *Do not overcook trout or any other fish.* Serve on a platter garnished with watercress and lemon wedges.

To eat Mr. Trout, pull out all fins with your fingers, then cut off, with your knife, a quarter inch of flesh down the back. Lift the fillets off with your knife on each side. But an old trout fisherman will probably say: "To hell with this, eat them with your fingers!"

BROILED TROUT

Here again, leave the heads and tails on and do not skin. Cover the bottom of an oven pan with melted butter, seasoning as for pan fried trout. Sprinkle a thin coating of bread crumbs on the bottom of the pan. Place the trout on its side. Sprinkle more crumbs on top together with some dry or fresh shredded parsley.

Set the oven at broil and when the trout are golden brown, turn off the broiler and set the oven heat to 450 degrees and cook 5 minutes more to slightly brown the bottom side of the fish.

To vary this recipe use marjoram, fresh basil or ground rosemary instead of the parsley. Each different herb will vary the taste delightfully.

TROUT ON THE GRILL

Place each trout on its own cut out piece of aluminum foil and season with salt and pepper, and 1 tablespoon of sherry. Put two pats of butter on top.

Close the foil tightly and put each "package" on the grill which should be 8 to 10 inches above the coals. Grill 4 to 5 minutes on each side, remove from the foil and serve, pouring the juices from each package over the trout.

A nice variation is to stuff each trout with a light bread stuffing or, better still, with fresh or canned crab meat.

TRUITE CANADIENNE (TROUT À LA CANADA)

I got this recipe from an old Indian guide on the North Shore of the Saint Lawrence River. He not only guided us but sometimes took over the cooking. He cooked trout outdoors in hot coals.

Sprinkle the inside of the trout with salt and pepper and place in it a piece of butter. Cut some orange slices and arrange on the back. Then wrap the trout tightly in aluminum foil, being sure to press all sides firmly. Put into the hot coals for about 15 minutes. (Or into a 350 degree oven). It's a delicious dish and so easy to do. Your friends will be properly impressed.

TRUITE EN PAPILLOTES
(TROUT IN PARCHMENT PAPER)

This exotic recipe was given me by Mr. J. J. Saunders, Kitchen Manager of Magdalene College, Cambridge, England. There's a bit of work in producing it but the results are magnificent!

4 6 to 8 oz. trout
½ small onion, minced
1 small can sliced
  mushrooms
1 tablespoon chopped
  parsley

2 tablespoons butter
Anchovy paste or
  finely chopped an-
  chovies
Salt and Pepper

Clean and bone the fish. Remove heads and tails. Sautè the minced onion, sliced mushrooms and parsley in the 2 tablespoons of butter until soft, not brown.

Make a thick white sauce and mix in the sautèd onion, mushrooms and parsley. Add to this a little anchovy paste (or chopped anchovies) and salt and pepper to taste. Allow this mixture to cool, then spread it all over the interior of the fish.

Fold the fish over and wrap each in a square of grease-proof paper which has been well oiled. Fold over the fish to make an envelope. Bake in a moderate oven for 15 to 20 minutes. Serves 4.

CREAMED TROUT A LA ELISABETH, PRINCESS
ALTENBURG

Wash, clean and dry the trout. Salt, then roll in fresh
cream and flour. Place in a long pyrex dish which has
been well buttered and brown on both sides (on top of the
stove). Then pour over a glass of port wine, a cup of
fresh cream. Bake in a medium oven for 5 minutes, basting often.

RAINBOW OR BROOK TROUT IN SOUR CREAM

This is a Swedish recipe that glorifies these delicious
fish.

*4 trout (8 to 12 inches   Flour
long)   4 tablespoons butter
Salt   ½ pint sour cream
Minced parsley*

Clean trout. Season with salt and pepper and dredge in
flour (or seasoned white corn meal). Sautè in butter
over high heat until brown on both sides. Then lower the
heat, add the sour cream and simmer for 5 minutes. Before serving, pour over the juices and garnish with chopped parsley and slices of lemon.

To complete a great treat serve with small boiled new
potatoes, green salad or green beans with slivered almonds. 4 portions.

TRUITE EN GELÉE (JELLIED TROUT)

Cook small trout "Au Bleue" (see page 142). Let cool,
then dry them. Meanwhile, add more salt to the water in
which the fish were boiled, put in a good shot of vinegar and an amount of gelatin needed for the quantity of
liquid. Pour ½ inch into a pyrex dish. After it has
jelled, place trout on top and pour the rest of the liquid
over.

When cooled and thoroughly jelled serve, garnished
with slices of hard boiled egg, dots of mayonnaise and
parsley.

TROUT IN WHITE WINE

4 trout	*Minced parsley*
Salt and pepper	*Vintage white wine*
4 medium sized onions,	*to cover*
minced	*Butter*
Breadcrumbs	

Poach trout in the white wine with the parsley and onions,
seasoning with salt and pepper. Cook slowly for 10 to 15
minutes. Remove the fish from the wine and place them
in an oven proof dish. Sprinkle lightly with breadcrumbs
and dot generously with butter. Place under the broiler
until brown. Serves 4.

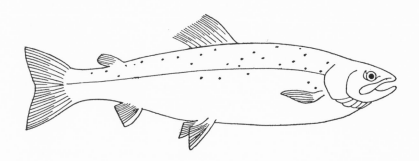

SALMON

Salmon has as great an appeal to the cook and the epicure as it has to the sport fisherman. Its firm flesh is rich and flavorful and "cooks up" beautifully in the skillet, the broiler, the oven or the boiling pot.

In parts of New England the Fourth of July celebration would be incomplete without salmon and green peas for dinner. It is as traditional as Saturday's baked beans, Thanksgiving turkey and Easter ham. At its best, of course, when freshly caught, it may be stuffed and baked, poached or cut into steaks and grilled, indoors or out. Served with green peas, picked that morning while the dew is still on the pods, it is a notable entrée.

BAKED STUFFED SALMON

(see Baked Stuffed Trout, page 143)

Wash and clean salmon. Boil 1 cup of white vinegar and pour over fish. This will cut the oily flavor.

Wrap the salmon in aluminum foil, tightening the ends. Preheat oven to 350 degrees and cook 15 to 20 minutes per pound. Unwrap, place on hot platter, skin and garnish with lemon slices, dill, parsley or watercress, the latter, if used, in one or more bunches. Serve with egg sauce or lemon butter (lemon juice mixed with melted butter). The size of the fish will determine the number of servings, allowing ½ pound per person.

SALMON STEAK CHORON À LA "21"

This is another fine recipe from M. Yves Louis Ploneis, Chef de Cuisine of the 21 Club, New York City. Simple but excellent.

Rub each salmon steak with oil and a little salt and pepper. Broil on each side for about 8 minutes. Serve each with an artichoke bottom filled with Béarnaise sauce and with grilled tomato slices. 1 steak (or more) per person.

SALMON WENBERG (SWEDISH)

Here is a really glorified creamed dish. The ingredients
below will make sufficient to serve 8 generously.

6 cups pre-cooked flaked   4 cups light cream (hot)
   salmon (or canned, if   3 teaspoons paprika
   necessary.)   1 teaspoon dry mustard
6 tablespoons flour   Salt and cayenne
8 tablespoons melted   pepper
   butter   6 egg yolks
5 tablespoons grated   5 tablespoons brandy
   Parmesan cheese   5 tablespoons sherry

Stir the 6 tablespoons of flour into the 8 tablespoons of
melted butter and cook over low heat for 2 or 3 minutes,
stirring constantly. Do not allow it to brown.

Slowly add 4 cups of hot (not boiled) light cream, stirring constantly, and cook sauce until it is thick and
smooth. Add the Parmesan cheese, paprika, dry mustard, salt and cayenne pepper to taste.

Beat the 6 egg yolks well in the top of a double boiler
and pour the sauce over them gradually, stirring as you
do it. Cook in double boiler for 3 minutes. Now add 5
tablespoons each of brandy and dry sherry and stir in
the 6 cups of salmon. Heat through.

Serve on toast points or crisp crackers. A tossed green
salad is a nice accompaniment.

SMOKED SALMON FINLANDIA

Your friends will swear this is real smoked salmon —
the best they've ever had! Interestingly enough, this is
the way it is processed and served in many of the best
restaurants and hotels.

Rub the raw fresh salmon on both sides with a mixture
of coarse salt and sugar (½ cup of coarse salt and ½ cup
of white sugar for each 4 to 4½ pounds). Put into a
stone crock, a deep Pyrex dish or any suitable bowl or
cooking utensil. Then place a board or a plate that fits
tightly into the dish so that it touches the salmon. Weigh
it down with a rock or other weight. Leave it for 36 hours,
turning it every 12 hours. When you take it out slice
it thinly across the grain, avoiding the skin. Serve raw
as is.

SALMON MOUSSE WITH DILL

The Swedes undoubtedly have a way with salmon. This recipe will make 2 one quart molds. Each mold will serve 4.

2 pounds skinned and
*   boned salmon*
4 eggs, well beaten
1 quart milk
¼ cup cornstarch
1 tablespoon salt
1 tablespoon mono-
*   sodium glutinate*
¾ teaspoon nutmeg

1 cup light cream
6 tablespoons fresh or
*   dried dill leaves*
¼ teaspoon tarragon
*   (optional)*
½ pound smoked
*   salmon*
6 teaspoons capers
*   (drained)*

Cut the fish into small cubes, pound it and strain through a sieve or, better yet purée it in a blender. Add the beaten eggs, milk, nutmeg, cornstarch, salt and monosodium glutinate, mixing a little at a time. Next add the cream and dill leaves (chopped fine) and blend in the blender for 30 seconds. (You will probably have to do this in several batches.) Now pour the mixture into 2 one quart molds, sprinkle each with bread crumbs and dot with butter.

Put the molds in a baking pan in 1 inch of boiling water and bake in a 325 degree oven for 55 minutes. Unmold onto a serving dish and sprinkle with finely chopped dill.

Serve hot with drawn butter sauce after garnishing it with rolled slices of smoked salmon, sprinkling each roll with ½ teaspoon of drained capers.

Addendum: If you do not need both molds at the same time you can freeze one of them right in the mold after it has cooled. Or unmold onto a baking sheet, wrap in freezer paper and put it into the freezer.

When you want to serve the frozen mousse let it stand for several hours until it has defrosted. (If wrapped for freezing put it back in the same mold it was cooked in.)

Sprinkle with bread crumbs, dot with butter and cover top of mold with foil. Put into baking pan in 1 inch of boiling water and cook in 325 degree oven for an hour. Garnish and serve as above.

SALMON LOAF

*1½ pounds pre-cooked
and flaked salmon
(or 1 large can)
½ cup fine bread
crumbs
4 tablespoons melted
butter
½ teaspoon salt*

*3 egg yolks, well beaten
1 teaspoon poultry
seasoning
1 tablespoon chopped
parsley
1 cup milk
3 egg whites well
beaten*

Mix the ingredients in the order given and steam in a mold for an hour. That's all there is to it! 3 or 4 servings.

SALMON SANDWICH DE LUXE

A grand luncheon dish, served with a light salad.

Remove the bones and flake 2 cups of cooked salmon (or 1 small can). Mix with 2 tablespoons horse radish, 1 tablespoon lemon juice, 4 tablespoons mayonnaise, salt and pepper. Spread generously between 2 slices of bread. (Trim off the crusts.) Then spread the outsides with butter and toast on both sides until golden brown.

Over the sandwiches pour the following sauce, piping hot: Melt 1 package of old English or cheddar cheese in the top of a double boiler and stir in ½ cup of milk.

SALMON BOUILLABAISSE FINLANDIA

The recipe of a true Finn, Lydia Kakko, this is a robust soup that can stand proudly beside any New England fish chowder, including Maine's cods' head chowder.

You will need 4 salmon (or grilse) heads, tails and fins. Remove the gills from the sides of the jawbones. This is very important.

Quarter 4 big potatoes, 1 medium onion, finely chopped, 1 cup chopped celery and some parsley. (Optional: add some rosemary and tarragon — but VERY SPARINGLY.)

Boil together for about 30 minutes in just enough water to cover. The potatoes will be almost done. Add ½ quart or more of cold milk and again bring to a boil. Then put in the fish heads, tails and fins and simmer for 5 minutes. Add 1 tablespoon of butter and season with salt and pepper to taste. This will serve 4.

You'll have to eat this with fork and spoon — and probably with your fingers too! It's strictly a family dish unless (Heaven forbid) you want to pick off all the meat in the kitchen and put it back into the soup to serve. It's my guess your friends, if they have been invited to share this great experience will feel as much at home as you do and dive in with fork, spoon and fingers.

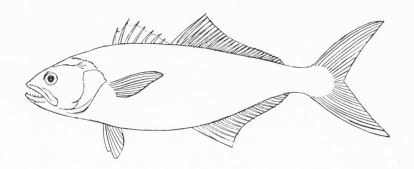

OTHER FISH

Fish recipes are largely interchangeable; thus you can use what fish comes to hand with successful results, plain or fancied up. For example, baked stuffed striped bass is as worthy as salmon, and perch can be cooked in any number of ways. And there are many, many other game fish, large and small, fresh or salt water, that lend themselves to the cooking methods herein.

SKILLET BASS IN BUTTER

Melt ½ cup of butter in a large skillet and arrange 6 two inch slices of bass in the pan. Cover each piece with a slice of tomato and squeeze the juice of 2 lemons over them. Salt and pepper to taste.

Now cover with a tight fitting lid and simmer for 20 minutes, basting often with the sauce in the pan. Serves 3.

STRIPED BASS AU COURT BOUILLON À LA "21"

From the repertoire of M. Yves Louis Ploneis, Chef de
Cuisine of the 21 Club, New York City.

1 striped bass (whole)	*1 cup water*
1 portion bouillon	*½ onion, minced*
½ cup wine	*1 carrot*
2 tablespoons white	*1 bay leaf*
vinegar	*1 clove garlic*
1 cup clear fish stock or	*Salt*

Make a broth of the above ingredients, cooking slowly
for ½ hour. Strain and pour over the bass and cook very
slowly for 20 minutes.

Meanwhile, slice in rings 4 small white onions and 2
small carrots and cook them separately from the fish.

When cooked pour over the bass. Chop parsley and sprinkle over. Serve very hot. The number of servings depends on size of fish.

PERCH WITH WINE SAUCE

3 pounds perch	*2 cloves*
3 cups water	*2 teaspoons salt*
1 cup white wine	*⅓ cup finely cut celery*
3 whole peppers	*2 diced carrots*
1 bay leaf	*1 sliced onion*
2 sprigs parsley	*2 tablespoons butter*

1½ tablespoons flour

Wash and clean fish well. Combine all the above ingredients except butter and flour. Bring to a boil and then put in the fish. Cook until fish is tender — about 25 minutes.

Remove fish to a hot platter. Strain the liquid in which it has cooked. Melt butter in a double boiler, add flour and stir until blended. Slowly add the cooking liquid, stirring constantly until the mixture thickens. If it is too thick to suit you add more wine. Pour over the fish and garnish with lemon quarters and sprigs of parsley. 4 to 6 servings.

STURGEON WITH LEMON DILL SAUCE

Sturgeon makes for wonderful eating but it's very hard to come by. The fish are generally very large, having been known to attain lengths of 10 to 12 feet and weights up to several hundred pounds. If you are lucky enough to catch one of these boneless wonders of pre-historic origin, or have a friend who wants to share his catch, by all means cook it this way.

Remove skin and cut large fillets. Rub them well with salt, pepper, monosodium glutinate and plenty of butter or margarine. Wrap each fillet in cooking foil or greased wax paper and bake in a 275 degree oven for 1 hour.

Serve with Lemon Dill Sauce (see page 196).

FISH SOUFFLÉ

Here are 3 ways of making fish soufflé, all excellent.

SOUFFLÉ NUMBER 1

This is simple to make and, in my experience, it has always come out well. The secret is to mix it in a blender and to use a slice of bread instead of a heavy white sauce.

1 cup of milk or white   *¼ teaspoon salt*
   wine   *¼ teaspoon nutmeg*
3 tablespoons butter   *1 cup cooked fish,*
1 slice white bread   *flaked*
1 teaspoon ready made   *5 egg yolks*
   mustard   *5 egg whites*
Paprika   *Parmesan cheese*

Heat the cup of milk or wine and 3 tablespoons of butter until the latter is melted. Pour into a blender, add 1 slice of white bread with the crust — all in pieces — ½ teaspoon ready made mustard, ¼ teaspoon salt and ¼ teaspoon nutmeg. Cover and blend for 5 seconds, then add 1 cup of finely flaked cooked fish and blend for 10 seconds.

Put in the 5 egg yolks and blend 15 seconds more. Beat the 5 egg whites until stiff but not dry and fold them in carefully with a rubber spatula. Butter a soufflé dish or oven proof, individual onion soup dishes.

Fill to within ½ inch of the top, sprinkle with Parmesan cheese and a little paprika, set on cooking sheet and bake in moderate preheated (375 degree) oven for 15 to 20 minutes until puffed and brown. Serve immediately. Serves 4.

SOUFFLÉ NUMBER 2

Mashed potatoes,   *Tomato slices*
  cooked rice or white   *Sour cream*
  cabbage leaves   *2 egg yolks*
Cooked fish (flaked)   *Lemon juice*
Sliced onion   *2 egg whites, beaten*

This is put together in layers and quantities will vary
with the size of your dish or by the amount of cooked fish
you have on hand.

Butter an ovenproof dish and cover bottom with a layer of mashed potatoes, cooked rice or white cabbage leaves (boiled or dried). Then place a layer of fish, in pieces, on top. Next a layer of softly cooked onions (cooked previously in butter) and some tomato slices. Then another layer of fish and a layer of onions and tomatoes. Last, make a thin layer of mashed potatoes or rice and cover with a mixture of sour cream, the egg yolks, salt, lemon juice and the well beaten egg whites. Bake in a 375 degree oven until golden brown. Serves 4.

SOUFFLÉ NUMBER 3

Onion rings   *2 to 4 eggs*
Cooked fish fillets   *Herbs*
2 to 3 tablespoons   *Parmesan cheese*
*   sour cream*   *Salt and pepper*

In a buttered oven proof dish place a layer of onion rings which have been softly cooked — but not browned — in oil. Cover with fillets of cooked trout, salmon, pike or most any other fish. Beat the eggs lightly and combine with the sour cream, salt, pepper and herbs (parlsey, dill, chives, tarragon or others of your choice). Pour the mixture over the fish, sprinkle with Parmesan cheese and bake in 375 degree oven until golden brown. Serves 4.

BRAISED SEAL FLIPPERS

These are a specialty of Mr. Ferry, Chef de Cuisine of the Mount Royal Club, Montreal, and were featured in the menu of the Grande Romaine Salmon Club Dinner which I extolled on page 13. The recipe will serve 24 but can be reduced for smaller groups! 1 flipper will do for 5 people.

6 seal flippers	*1 cup chopped leeks*
Juice of 2 lemons	*Parsley*
Flour	*Bay Leaf*
2 cups chopped onions	*Consommé*
1 cup chopped celery	*1 can stewed tomatoes*
1 cup diced carrots	*2 cups white wine*

Salt and pepper

Skin flippers and clean off fat. Parboil for 2 hours in water and lemon juice. Dredge with flour. Sauté in fat until brown and place in a pan or saucepan for braising.

Add the onions, celery, carrots, leeks, parsley and bay leaf. Cover with consommé, the stewed tomatoes, the wine and salt and pepper. Braise until tender, then remove and place on serving dish.

Strain the sauce and add 1 glass sherry. Thicken the sauce with a roux (butter and flour).

Garnish the flippers with 1 pound each of sautéd mushrooms, sautéd silver onions and marble potatoes. Cover all with the sauce and serve with mashed turnips.

FROGS' LEGS QUÉBÉCOISE

While frogs are finless they are amphibians and more in the water than out. So I've included them with fish.

For a fun experience take your best girl frog hunting some warm moonlit summer night along a meandering country brook. Catch some frogs but don't be such an eager beaver that you devote all your attention to the frogs.

To prepare the frogs for cooking sever the legs just above the hips. Some people clean the whole frog for eating but to me it's a waste of time and effort. Cut the feet off at the ankle joint and peel the skin off the legs. (It usually pulls off like a pair of stretch pants.)

Now separate each leg, wash in cold water, salt them lightly and place in the refrigerator overnight.

To cook, dip in flour seasoned with salt, pepper and garlic. (THIS IS A MUST.) Fry until golden brown in a skillet greased with half cooking oil and half butter.

To eat, use your fingers. And enjoy!

GAME SOUPS

There are any number of delicious soups to be made from odds and ends of game, including the bones and innards. And many of them can take on the character of stews if you add enough vegetables and potatoes and rice.

Those I have included in the following pages are particularly good: they have been favorites of mine for many years.

GAME SOUP À LA DIANE

¾ pound leftover game   4 cups water
   meat   1 shake ginger, thyme
4 parsley or celery roots   and nutmeg
5 carrots   ½ bay leaf
4 onions, chopped   ¼ pound butter
Salt   4 tablespoons flour
10 whole peppercorns   1 cup red wine
1 teaspoon whole mixed   ½ cup port wine
   pickling spices   (optional)
                  1 cup cream

This is a most substantial soup — a rib-sticker, if you know what I mean.

Cut the carrots and roots into thin slices and simmer in fat until golden brown. Add the onion and simmer until soft. Cut the meat into small pieces and add together with water, salt and other spices, simmering until everything is soft.

Remove the meat and mince half of it very, VERY fine like a purée. Leave the other half in small pieces.

Mix flour with a little water and add to the other ingredients in the pot. Boil for at least 30 minutes over moderate heat. Now pass it through a sieve, pour in the red wine, the port wine and cream. Heat — but do not boil — then put the meat purée and the meat pieces back in and serve immediately. 6 to 8 servings.

CLEAR GAME SOUP

Game bones (any kind)	*1 cup beef bouillon*
1 cup game meat	*1 teaspoon salt*
2 carrots	*½ teaspoon paprika*
1 onion, minced	*¼ teaspoon nutmeg*
1 tablespoon minced parsley	*6 bouillon cubes*
	6 cups water
⅛ teaspoon sage	*1 tablespoon chopped celery*

Cut the bones as small as possible and fry quickly in fat with the carrots and herbs until brown. Add water, salt, and minced onions and simmer over low heat for several hours.

Sieve the soup but be sure that no small bones fall in it—especially those of birds. The best method is through cheese cloth.

Season with salt, a little paprika, a pinch of nutmeg and herbs. Add a bouillon cube. Put in some noodles or rice, a small amount of game meat cut into strips, or dumplings or raw lightly beaten eggs. Serves 6.

HUNTER'S SOUP

For this you boil leftovers of hare including the bones. Add brownly fried bones of any other game and simmer for several hours (in enough water to cover). Remove the bones, cut off the meat and put through a grinder. Add frankfurters cut in slices or fried sausages, sliced and put all the meat into a soup tureen. Pour over the sieved liquid in which the game was cooked, season to taste, and garnish with chives or bread squares that have been roasted in butter.

Hunters' Toast: Use home baked or other coarse grained bread. Cut in fairly thick slices, butter generously on one side only and toast over flame, buttered side up.

BEAVER TAIL SOUP

If you recall, this soup was served at the memorable dinner of the Grande Romaine Salmon Club (see page 13).

It is a creation of Mr. Ferry, Chef de Cuisine of the Mount Royal Club, Montreal, and his specifications below will produce enough soup to serve 24 people.

1 gallon consommé   *2 pounds cut up*
1 small beaver   *vegetables (carrots,*
1 cup sherry   *onions, celery, leeks)*

Cut off the tail of the beaver and wrap it in cheese cloth.

Cut up the beaver into small pieces and blanch. All fat and musk glands must be removed (2 on top of back, 2 on each of the front paws).

In a large skillet cook in fat the beaver and vegetables until the meat is browned. Strain off the fat. Add the beaver meat, vegetables and the wrapped, uncooked tail to the consommé and simmer for 5 hours. Strain, keep the tail. Clarify the stock with the whites of 12 eggs and 2 cups of water. Put in the skinned and diced beaver tail and pre-cooked, very finely diced carrots and celery (¼ cup each). Season to taste. This soup can be frozen and kept for 6 months or given to your favorite neighbors!

ENGLISH HARE SOUP

Fry the forelegs, neck, head, etc. in fat with 2 minced onions, until brown. Add 1 bay leaf, thyme, chopped parsley, a can of bouillon or clear game soup. Let simmer until the meat is done.

Remove the meat and cut from the bones. Slice or cut it into squares and put in a soup tureen. (Keep it warm.)

Now prepare a thick, brown sauce, thin it with the hot soup and add 2 glasses of sweet white wine, a little cayenne pepper, salt and bouillon cube. Pour over the meat in the tureen. Serve with small, buttered squares of white bread. It is a lovely supper dish which will serve 6.

HUNGARIAN GAME SOUP

1 large onion, minced	*1 tablespoon lemon*
½ teaspoon sweet	*juice*
paprika	*½ teaspoon caraway*
1 can consommé	*seeds*
A little flour	*1 bouillon cube*
1 pint water	*½ teaspoon sugar*

Salt

Cut a cup or more of any game meat into hazelnut size. Brown the onion in fat and when brown add ½ teaspoon sweet paprika, 1 cup of water or 1 cup of consommé and simmer with the meat until tender (several hours).

Add a little flour and more paprika, a little lemon juice, a few caraway seeds, a bouillon cube, a pinch of sugar and salt. Garnish with chopped parsley.

QUAIL OR WOODCOCK POTAGE

This is an excellent way of using badly shot birds.

½ cup barley or brown rice	glutinate
	½ teaspoon celery salt
1 teaspoon monosodium	Salt and pepper

Place four cleaned birds in a boiling kettle with 8 cups of water. Simmer gently for two hours over low heat. Strain the broth, then pick the meat from the bones and grind with a meat grinder or chop very fine.

Place the meat in the broth, bring to a boil and add ½ cup of barley or brown rice (barley requires longer cooking time) and cook until barley or rice is tender. Season with 1 level teaspoon of monosodium glutinate or any good mixed spice, a shake of celery salt and salt and pepper to taste. Serves 8 generously.

WILD GAME GUMBO
(AGAIN FOR BADLY SHOT BIRDS)

For 10 servings place in a stewing pan with sufficient water to cover 1 dressed pheasant, 4 dressed quail or 1 chicken or any other combination of game you may have, and simmer slowly until tender. While simmering add 1 bay leaf, 1 small onion, a stalk of celery, salt and pepper.

Remove the carcasses from the broth and strain the broth into another kettle. Cut meat from the bones and chop fine. Add one half of the meat to the broth. (Save the remainder for sandwiches, salad or to use in any way you see fit.)

Now add:

1 scraped carrot	*1 green pepper,*
2 stalks of celery	*chopped*
chopped	*1 onion, chopped*
1 can of chopped tomatoes with juice	

This is now your basic soup and you are ready for the refinements.

Place the basic soup in a double boiler and add 1 can of green pea soup or 1 package of dried green pea soup and 1 pound of your favorite boned and skinned fish (in New Orleans red snapper is preferred).

*1 cup deveined, cut
up shrimp
1 cup crab meat
2 level teaspoons mono-
sodium glutinate*

*1 level teaspoon
whole thyme
Salt and pepper
1 heaping teaspoon
of Gumbo filé**

Serve this flavorful soup piping hot with rice and make a meal of it! It's so-o-o good!

If you reheat it be sure it's a double boiler.

PURÉE OF GAME SOUP

Either prepare a clear game soup (see page 173) or use one or two bouillon cubes in water. Put a few peppercorns, juniper berries, 1 bay leaf and a cup or more of diced carrots, turnips, celery and leeks. Simmer until they are soft. Add tomato paste, 1 or 2 cups of minced or cooked ground game, a little rice, herbs, a piece of fresh butter and a little sherry. Reheat and sprinkle with chopped chives.

Fry small squares of bread in butter until brown and serve separately.

*(This is a spice much used in the Bayou country, a combination of powdered marjoram and sassafras leaves which is the secret of a good bouillabaisse.)

LA SOUPE AUX POIS

It is an axiom of gastronomy that in the design of the Universe, a great Divinity abundantly provided for the health and happiness of mankind. He gave to all the peoples of the world, each in their climate, instinctive knowledge of nutrition and peculiar skill in preparing esculants indigenous to their native lands. Hence to the genius of the Canadian "Habitant" is attributed a priceless treasure admired of all epicures, a culinary masterpiece famed for sapidity and succulence, an Ambrosia worthy of a Dyonysian Agape. Its simple and immortal name is

HABITANT PEA SOUP*

1 gallon water	*1 pig shank or ham*
2 pounds fried whole	*bone*
yellow peas	*2 Spanish onions*
2 pounds salt pork	*6 slices raw lean*
3 carrots	*bacon*

In 3 gallon cauldron put 1 gallon of water, 2 pounds of fried whole yellow peas, a flat section of salt pork weighing 2 pounds, deeply scored across the top, and a pig shank (the hock) with the skin removed. Let stand overnight.

Add 3 large carrots, scraped, halved and wrapped in cheese cloth to facilitate removal. Also, 2 Spanish onions, skinned, halved and similarly bound.

*While this is a game cook book I have added this delicious soup because it complements game and fish and is loved by every sportsman I've ever known.

Place over the fire, bring to a boil then turn low to simmer for 3 hours, covered. At the end of that time add six slices of raw, lean bacon to insure a smoky flavor, and boil again, uncovered, for 1 hour.

Remove the salt pork, hock, carrots, onions and bacon.

Season with salt and mustard. NEVER STRAIN SOUPE AUX POIS or remove the pea husks. Serve hot in terracotta bowls.

This is the way Joe Legault of St. Polycarpe, Quebec, makes Habitant soup and there is none better! Serves 10.

COURT BOUILLON À LA "21"

This is the way it's made by M. Yves Louis Ploneis, Chef de Cuisine of the 21 Club, New York City.
Make a broth of:

½ cup dry white wine	½ onion, minced
2 tablespoons white vinegar	1 carrot
	1 bay leaf
1 cup clear fish stock or 1 cup water	1 clove
	½ clove of garlic

Salt

Cook slowly for ½ hour. Strain over fish and simmer 10 or 20 minutes until done.

FISH CHOWDER

Fish chowder is not indigenous to New England and
Nova Scotia as Yankee and Bluenose boasters would have
us believe. It came to us from Brittany where, for centuries,
it has been the dish of welcome to Breton fishermen return-
ing home after weeks — even months — at sea.

Traditionally, as the fleet hove into view, the wives and
sweethearts rushed to the shore to light a fire under a huge,
iron cauldron already filled with water. At the sight of the
dancing flames a resounding cheer of anticipation, such as
could come only from men who had not had a hot meal since
leaving port, would go up from the fleet. Followed, when the
little vessels came within earshot, by *"Faites la chaudière,"*
"Faites la chaudière!" (Make the soup kettle ready.)

For answer the womenfolk held aloft the platters of potatoes, onions and carrots they had been slicing and then ceremoniously added them, along with generous chunks of salt
pork, to the now boiling water.

Less ceremoniously, the moment their craft were made
fast, the fishermen leaped ashore to greet their loved ones
with an ardor that bespoke their long celibacy. Then, as
though paying forfeit for the additional due he would shortly
claim, each man tossed a well cleaned fish — the prize of his
catch — into the steaming court bouillon.

Thus as a living language never stands still, the French *chaudière* has become our chowder. And what a delightful heritage it is!

NEW ENGLAND FISH CHOWDER

Over the years refinements have been added to the original Brittany chowder. This particular recipe was given to a friend by Mrs. Jacqueline Kennedy, then living in the White House.

2 lbs. Haddock or any	*1 bay leaf, crumbled*
other white fish	*1 quart milk*
2 oz. salt pork, diced	*2 tablespoons butter*
4 large potatoes, diced	*1 teaspoon salt*
1 cup chopped celery	*Freshly ground pepper*
2 onions, sliced	

Simmer the fish in 2 cups of water for 15 minutes. Drain.

Reserve the broth. Remove the bones from the fish.

In the chowder pot sautè diced salt pork until crisp.

Remove pork dice and set aside. Sauté the onions in the pork fat until golden brown. Add the fish, potatoes, celery, bay leaf, salt and pepper. Pour in the fish broth and enough boiling water to make 3 cups of liquid. Simmer for 30 minutes. Add the milk and butter and simmer for 5 minutes more.

Serve the chowder sprinkled with the pork dice. 6 servings.

CHOWDER "DELUGE"

You might like this type of chowder. It breaks several of
the rules for an authentic New England chowder but not
as radically as others I've tasted.

1½ lbs. saltwater fish	*3 tablespoons olive oil*
(haddock, perch, cod,	*1½ cups consommé*
eel)	*or water*
1 large onion, chopped	*1½ cups tomato juice*
2 stalks celery, chopped	*1 teaspoon salt*
3 potatoes, diced	*1 shake of Tabasco*
2 carrots, diced	*2 cups milk*

Chopped parsley or chopped salted peanuts

In the chowder pot heat the oil, add the onion and celery
and cook over low heat for 10 minutes. Add the potatoes, carrots, tomato juice, consommé or water, salt and
Tabasco. Bring to a boil then reduce heat, cover tightly
and simmer for 25 minutes, or until the vegetables are
tender.

Remove any skin from the fish and cut into 1 inch pieces.
Add to the pot when the vegetables are tender. Simmer
for another 10 minutes. Add the milk and heat but do
not allow it to boil. Serve with a little chopped parsley
or chopped salted peanuts. 6 servings.

You can prepare this ahead of time but don't add the milk
until you're ready to serve.

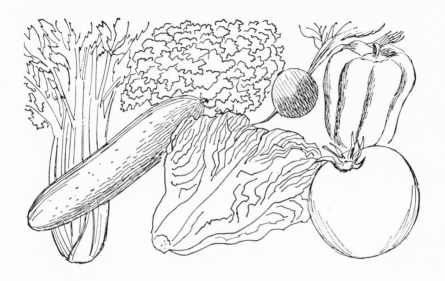

SALADS

From the simplest of tossed green salads to the most elaborate combinations of legumes and fruits, not forgetting the jellied creations, the salad repertory is extensive. I am sure you have, in your recipe file, a considerable number of favorites, as I have. And, of course, you have favorites among the many dressings.

Thus I shall not attempt to catalog a large number of salads. Suffice it to say that there are few, if any, that do not complement game and add zest to its enjoyment, your own productions included. Those I have detailed below are on my "preferred-with-game list." They are comparatively simple, utilizing a variety of greens and vegetables as well as grapefruit and orange segments with dressings on the tart side. You may like them too.

GARDEN SALAD

As the friend of mine who gave me this recipe said, "It's
a very light salad to serve with heavy game. Cool and
crisp, it is loaded with vitamins and not the least bit fat-
tening." The quantities below will serve 4.

1 large onion   *1 cup vinegar*
1 large green pepper   *2 cups water*
2 medium tomatoes   *1 tablespoon sugar*
2 stalks of celery   *1 level teaspoon black*
1 large cucumber   *pepper*
                  1 level teaspoon salt

Peel the cucumber and remove the eye stem from the
tomatoes. Chop these and the other vegetables into ½
inch chunks and place in a salad bowl. Add vinegar,
water, sugar, pepper and salt and stir thoroughly. Place
the bowl in the refrigerator to chill well. Serve in individual bowls, spooning some of the liquid over each.

SPRING SALAD

Here is a combination of greens and vegetables that really celebrates Spring!
The ingredients:

Endive	*Green spring onions*
Iceberg lettuce	*Green pepper*
Bibb lettuce	*Celery*
Escarole	*Red Cabbage*
Radishes	*Parmesan cheese*

This salad calls for your own creativeness in the quantities of each you use. And the number of people you are to serve.

After washing the leafy vegetables and shaking off excess water, place them in the refrigerator the day before, covering them with paper towels. When ready to put the salad together cut or tear the leaves into reasonably sized pieces and place them in the salad bowl. Sliver the radishes and cut up the green onions. The addition of chopped green pepper, celery and red cabbage is optional—but I recommend it highly.

Just before serving add your favorite dressing (mine's on page 194, She Dressing), sprinkle generously with Parmesan cheese and toss lightly.

CAESAR'S OR HE-MAN'S SALAD

The Spring Salad above is the basis for this salad. Add a small amount of crumbled Roquefort or Blue cheese and ten or twelve croutons for each serving. If you wish, sprinkle on Romano cheese or a combination of Romano and Parmesan. The Romano is stronger which might suit your taste. In making your dressing (it should be French) use white vinegar: it is sharper.

To make the croutons: Toast cubed bread slowly until golden brown and dry. This is best done with oven heat rather than under the broiler. Dip each crouton into olive oil in which a clove of garlic has been mashed. Remove croutons quickly and give them a coating of Parmesan cheese, then add them to the salad. (Frankly, I could make a meal of these croutons!)

SALAD BASCOM

The basic salad is composed of 4 greens whose color contrast is as appealing to the eye as the finished result is to the taste buds. They are

Tender leaf lettuce *Fresh spinach leaves*
Bibb lettuce *Endive with white
center*

Wash the greens thoroughly, shake off excess water and place in the refrigerator overnight covered with paper towels. Break the leaves into small pieces with your fingers and place all in a salad bowl.

Now comes the time to mix in any or all of the following:

Chopped spring onions *Diced green pepper*
Slices of red radishes *Diced tender celery*

A word of caution: Don't use too much of these ingredients — an overload will make the salad heavy. And *never* use carrots.

With all the above in the salad bowl, add a very liberal amount of grated Parmesan cheese. Now toss well to mix the cheese and the greens. Finally, spoon on Italian Pepper dressing (see page 194) and toss thoroughly again.

GRAPEFRUIT SALAD

This is particularly good with game birds — pheasant, quail, partridge and duck.

2 seedless grapefruit   *4 scallions, minced*
Boston lettuce   *(use the white and a*
¼ cup French dressing   *little of the green)*
Black pepper

Shred the lettuce and place an amount on each salad plate. Cover completely with perfect segments of grapefruit. (Remove the membranes.) Sprinkle lightly with the minced scallions. Pour on just enough French dressing to moisten and sprinkle with black pepper. 4 to 6 servings.

ORANGE AND ONION SALAD

You can make this in two ways: 1) with fresh orange segments and thin slices of Bermuda onion (or any mild onion) or 2) with canned Mandarin oranges and canned French fried onion rings. Either way it is a scrumptious gastronomic foil for all kinds of game.

Method 1.

Peel the oranges, ½ orange per person, and separate into segments. Be sure to remove the membranes. Slice the onion into thin slices. Allow 1 to 2 sizable onions to 4 oranges, depending on your taste. Be generous with the amount of lettuce you put into the bottom of the salad bowl. Tear it into pieces. Then bed down the orange segments and onion slices. Refrigerate until ready to serve. Just before serving pour over a *sharp* French dressing and toss well.

Method 2.

Drain the Mandarin orange sections. Follow the same procedure as above, bedding down the orange sections but do not add the French fried onion rings until ready to serve. Then pour on the dressing and toss.

SHE DRESSING FOR GREEN SALADS

2 parts olive oil   *1 part white vinegar*
1 large clove garlic   *Black pepper*
                    Salt

To the olive oil in which the garlic clove has been mashed, add the vinegar, a liberal amount of black pepper and salt to taste. Allow the mixture to set for at least an hour before using. A grand old French chef, famous for his salads, among other things, told me "always use enough salt for dressings."

ITALIAN PEPPER DRESSING

⅓ cup white or malt   *1 teaspoon salt*
vinegar   *2 cloves garlic*
1 level teaspoon black   *⅔ cup virgin olive*
pepper   *oil*

Place the vinegar in a mixing jar. Add the level teaspoon of black pepper and the teaspoon of salt. Squash 2 cloves of garlic into the vinegar and add the olive oil. Let it set for at least a half hour before using so that the pepper and garlic flavors will permeate the olive oil. (Note on olive oil: quality varies considerably. Be sure you use oil from virgin runs.)

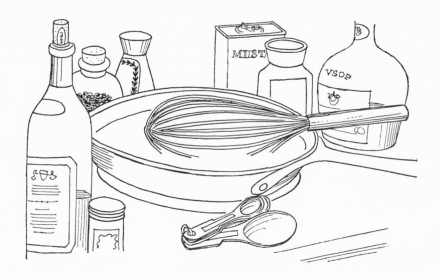

SAUCES

"Sharpen with cloyless sauce his appetite"

—*William Shakespeare*

Sauces are perhaps more important for game than for any other meat. While the inherent dryness of the meat can be relieved to a large extent by proper larding, it is the sauce that will develop fully its delicate flavor and succulence. No sauce or gravy should disguise or smother natural savoriness: it should complement it agreeably. Thus herbs and other seasonings, sour cream or buttermilk, wines or cognac, jellies, syrups or juices or other ingredients must be chosen, combined and blended carefully.

I am, as you have probably guessed, a sauce exponent and those I have included here are, in my opinion, the most appropriate accents for game of various kinds.

LEMON AND DILL SAUCE

¼ pound butter
1 heaping tablespoon
    flour
½ cup water

Juice of 2 lemons
1 level teaspoon dill
⅛ teaspoon citric acid
    (sour salt)

Salt and pepper

In a double boiler melt the butter and stir in the flour until blended. Now add ½ cup of water, the lemon juice, dill, citric acid, salt and white pepper. Cook over low heat until the mixture is thick and hot.

It can be used for all fish. Pour over fillets on serving platter and sprinkle with paprika and parsley flakes. Makes about 1 cup.

SAUCE ESPAGNOLE

3 carrots	*1 tablespoon flour*
1 onion	*Stock to moisten*
Butter	*Bouquet of herbs or*
Scraps of game	*wild game seasoning*

Cut up the carrots and onion and put them in a skillet with a little butter. Add immediately any scraps of game and, if available, some veal bones. Cover and cook over low heat until pale brown then stir in the flour and enough hot stock to moisten. Stir constantly until it thickens. Finally add a bouquet of herbs or wild game seasoning and simmer for 1 hour.

Strain to serve. You can prepare this sauce before hand as it will keep for a week if put into a tightly covered jar and refrigerated.

HOLIDAY SAUCE

For rabbit, squirrel, ground hog or similar game.

1½ sticks butter
2 tablespoons flour
1 small can crushed
    pineapple with juice
1 can (small) seedless
    black cherries with
    juice
Salt

1 deseeded orange,
    cut into segments,
    skin and all
1 cup sweet red wine
    such as muscatel
2 tablespoons sugar
1½ level teaspoons
    curry powder

Place the butter in a double boiler. When melted add the flour and stir until blended. Add the remaining rabbit (or other game) broth from the pan and all other ingredients. Cook over hot water until the sauce thickens. (Stir it constantly.) As a final fillip stir in 1 jigger of bourbon whiskey or rum and pour, piping hot, over the game.

Makes 2 cups.

BREAD SAUCE

Skin a small onion and stud it with 3 whole cloves. Place in a saucepan with 2 cups of milk and bring to a boil.

Add 3 cups of fine, dry bread crumbs. Then place over hot (not boiling) water to permit the crumbs to absorb the milk. Discard the onion. Beat the mixture with a fork, seasoning with ¾ teaspoon salt and ¼ teaspoon paprika.

The sauce should be medium — not thick or thin. Add 2 tablespoons of butter. Use either more bread crumbs or more milk to arrive at the proper consistency. 2 cups.

SAUCE REMOULADE

To 2 or 3 tablespoons of mayonnaise add a few drops of soup seasoning, 1 tablespoon of capers, minced, or dill pickles, finely chopped, a little grated onion, 1 or 2 table-spoons of red wine and ½ cup strained game sauce or stock. Finally, add a bit of mustard, salt, a pinch or two of sugar, lemon juice and pepper and mix well. 1 cup.

MUSTARD-DILL SAUCE

4 egg yolks	*1 teaspoon sugar*
2 tablespoons dry mustard	*2 cups olive oil*
	4 tablespoons vinegar
2 teaspoons French mustard	*4 tablespoons chopped fresh or dried dill*

Beat the egg yolks until lemon colored. Add the mustard, salt and sugar. Mix well. Pour in the olive oil very slowly, beating while you add it until the mixture reaches the thickness of gravy. Then beat in the vinegar and the chopped dill. 2½ cups. For a *Good Lemon-Mustard Sauce* omit the vinegar and dill and use instead 4 tablespoons of lemon juice. I had this at the American Pavilion at the New York World's Fair and it was excellent.

SOUR CREAM SAUCE

This is particularly good with venison!

2 tablespoons butter	2 peppercorns,
2 tablespoons flour	crushed fine
2 shallots, chopped	1 cup sour cream
4 tablespoons white	Juice of ½ lemon
wine	Salt

Pour off excess fat from the pan in which the venison was cooked. Melt the butter in the pan, stir in the flour and shallots and blend well being sure to mix in all the brown fat in the pan. Add, slowly, the wine and peppercorns, stirring as you add them. Finally add the sour cream and a little salt and pepper. Cook, stirring continually until thickened. Strain through sieve. 1½ cups.

Before serving add the lemon juice. Pour over the meat.

WILD DUCK BASTING SAUCE

6 oranges   1 teaspoon lemon
Orange rinds   juice
1 cup brown sugar   ½ cup dark rum

Squeeze the juice from the 6 oranges. Cut the rind into strips, cover with water and simmer for 30 minutes. Drain. Cover with fresh water and simmer again for 30 minutes. Drain. Cover with fresh water and simmer again for 30 minutes. Drain and once more cover with water, add the brown sugar, lemon juice and orange juice. Cook until the rind is tender to the fork.

Pour into the blender, add the rum and blend until smooth. (It should resemble a thick paste.) 2 cups.

COLD ORANGE SAUCE

6 tablespoons currant   2 tablespoons lemon
   jelly   juice
3 tablespoons sugar   3 tablespoons port
2 orange rinds, grated   wine
2 tablespoons orange   Salt and pepper
   juice   Paprika

Beat the jelly, sugar and rind in a mixer. Add the remaining ingredients and mix. Serve cold with any game.

(The sauce can be stored in the refrigerator.) 1 cup.

SAUCE VELOUTÉ

2 tablespoons butter	*2 cups milk or*
2 tablespoons flour	*2 cups fish stock*

Salt and pepper

Melt the butter over low heat. Blend in the flour and cook slowly, stirring constantly. Do not allow the mixture to brown. Remove from heat and add either 2 cups of milk or 2 cups of fish stock. Beat with a wire whisk until smooth. Return to moderate heat and stir until the mixture comes to a boil, then allow it to cook for 1 minute. Season with salt and pepper. 2 cups.

FRENCH GAME SAUCE

Mix together 1 cup of thinned wine vinegar (half water), 1 clove of garlic, mashed, 1 chopped hare liver and 1 cup of hare's blood (substitute 1 slice of calf's liver if hare's liver and blood are not available). Press through a sieve, add left over gravy, salt, pepper, a pinch of thyme, Gravy Brown and plenty of fresh green celery leaves, minced. Heat well in a double boiler 20 to 30 minutes.

EGG SAUCE FOR FISH

2 raw eggs	*⅓ cup white vinegar*
1 hard boiled egg,	*1 tablespoon flour*
chopped	*1 tablespoon butter*

1 cup milk

Beat the raw eggs with the vinegar until smooth. Blend the butter and flour, add the milk and heat to the boiling point. Remove from heat and beat the egg mixture into the white sauce with a wire whisk. Place over low heat and stir until it thickens.

Finally beat in another tablespoon of butter, add the hard boiled egg, sprinkle with parsley or dill. Serve separately in a gravy boat.

WARM MAYONNAISE

A very delicate sauce much favored by fish connoisseurs!

1 tablespoon butter	*2 to 3 tablespoons*
1 tablespoon flour	*mayonnaise*
Fish stock, dry white	*Vinegar*
wine or lemon juice	*1 tablespoon chopped*
Salt	*parsley*

1 tablespoon chopped dill

Blend the butter and flour as for a white sauce. Add the fish stock, white wine or lemon juice which has been mixed with the mayonnaise. Do not boil. It should be good and warm.

Season with a little salt and vinegar. If you want more color add chopped herbs, a very finely chopped pickle or chopped capers, ground lemon rind or a little tomato meat that is not too wet.

MUSTARD BUTTER

In a sauce pan melt ½ cup butter. Remove from heat and add 1 teaspoon lemon juice and ¼ teaspoon salt. Beat in gradually 2½ teaspoons prepared mustard. Continue beating until the sauce is thick and cool. Serve slightly chilled with fish or grilled meat.

TARRAGON BUTTER

Blanch 4 tablespoons of fresh tarragon leaves and rinse with cold water. Pound the leaves to a pulp and cream them thoroughly with ½ cup of softened butter and 1 tablespoon of lemon juice. Force the mixture through a very fine strainer. Serve with fish or fowl.

CURRY SAUCE

Mix ½ to 1 teaspoon of curry powder and a little leftover game gravy into a small amount of white sauce.

HORSERADISH PAPRIKA SAUCE

Into a very thick game gravy put ½ teaspoon sweet paprika, a full tablespoon of minced horseradish, 1 to 2 tablespoons of finely chopped almonds and 2 to 3 tablespoons of sweet cream. Season to taste with sugar, salt and Bisto.

MUSTARD SAUCE

Add 1 cup of mayonnaise, 2 to 3 teaspoons of mustard, a pinch of sugar, salt, pepper and minced herbs to 1 cup of cold game gravy from which the fat has been skimmed.

SAUCE CUMBERLAND

For each person stir in a cup 1 tablespoon of mustard, 1 tablespoon of red currant jelly, 1 tablespoon of oil or mayonnaise, a little lemon and orange juice, grated lemon rind and orange peel, salt and pepper.

SWEDISH APPLE SAUCE

Stew sour apples in a little water until soft. Pass them through a sieve. Add thick game gravy, minced onion, salt, a little sugar and Bovril. Serve hot or cold.

RED WINE MARINADE

Boil 4 pints of lightly salted water with carrots, celery, onions, mixed spice, juniper berries, thyme, marjoram and whole peppers. Simmer for several hours then add 1 pint of vinegar and 1 pint of red wine. When this has come to a boil, let it cool. Pour over the game and leave for not more than 4 days. If there is not enough fluid to cover, turn the meat every 12 hours.

MILK MARINADE

Use fresh, skimmed or, better still, buttermilk. Cover
the meat completely. Turn once or twice every day. If
fresh milk is used, change the milk every second day. (No
change is necessary if you use buttermilk.) Do not leave
longer than 4 to 6 days. When ready to cook, wash and
dry the meat well.

SOYA STEAK MARINADE

*3 five ounce bottles
   soya sauce
1 teaspoon powdered
   or fresh ginger*

*2 tablespoons brown
   sugar
¼ cup wine*

This is particularly good for gamey steaks. Meat may
be soaked overnight in or out of the refrigerator for 4 to
6 hours before cooking. The steaks should be turned occasionally. The above quantities are enough for 4 to 6
small steaks or 1 large thick steak.

NATURAL GAME GRAVY

Put your roast into HOT fat together with cut up onions. Turn the meat quickly so that it browns on all sides and the pores close. If the fat is too cool, the juices will run out and the meat as well as the gravy won't get brown.

When the meat is well browned slowly pour water over the top and repeat (or use canned bouillon, buttermilk or sour cream). The gravy will brown nicely if you follow this procedure of pouring the water slowly.

When the roast has 30 minutes to cook (in the oven) add sliced carrots, leeks and onions (not obligatory).

A piece of dark bread will help too. After you have removed the roast from the pan, sprinkle flour into the gravy and stir constantly for 5 minutes. Strain into a gravy boat for serving.

ANCHOVY SAUCE

Add to the above anchovy paste, half a ground sour apple, a pinch of sugar and minced parsley.

VEGETABLES

The subject of vegetables — their selection, preparation, cooking and serving — is entirely too voluminous for a book like this. You might say that, were I to include even a partial compendium, it would be like the tail wagging the dog. What goes with other meat, fowl, and fish goes equally as well with the game varieties.

There are, however, just a few I want to share with you. They are on the unusual side and I have found them particularly good with game.

RED CABBAGE WITH APPLES

1 medium head red
   cabbage
1 or 2 tart apples
2 tablespoons chicken
   or bacon fat
1 medium onion,
   sliced
1 quart water
½ cup light vinegar
   (red wine vinegar

   preferred)
½ cup sugar
½ teaspoon salt
¼ teaspoon pepper
2 cloves
Juice of ½ lemon
1 bay leaf
2 or 3 tablespoons
   flour

Wash the cabbage and drain. Cut up as for cole slaw. Wash and core the apples, peel and cut into small pieces.

Heat the fat in a large sauce pan and sauté the onion and apples for 3 or 4 minutes. Add the water, vinegar, sugar, salt, pepper, cloves, bay leaf and lemon juice. Stir and bring to a boil. Add the cabbage.

Cover and simmer for 45 minutes or until tender. Just before serving sprinkle flour on top to absorb liquid. Serves 4 to 6.

CHAMPAGNE SAUERKRAUT SURPRISE

When you buy the pineapple for this try to get a female fruit. It is distinguished by little pineapple buds all around the crown and is tender and sweeter than the male fruit, as are most females!

2 pounds fresh sauer-
kraut
(I never buy it in
cans!)
2 cups water
1 fresh pineapple

(or 1 apple)
3 tablespoons bacon fat
2 tablespoons chopped
onion
1 cup champagne or
dry white wine

Put the sauerkraut in an enamel pot and stir with a fork so the air can get through. Cut off the top of the pineapple about an inch down. (You will have to use the empty pineapple shell for serving so it will be necessary to cut out the meat by running a knife down and around after you have cut the bottom off about ½ inch up. You should have a nice circular piece.) Now slice into thin slices. (If you use an apple, peel it, core it and slice thin.)

Place a layer of pineapple between two layers of sauerkraut. Add the water, cover tightly. Simmer for ½ hour.

Meanwhile glaze the onion in bacon fat until soft, not brown. Add to the sauerkraut and simmer ¼ hour more. Sauerkraut is good if cooked the day before and warmed up.

Add the champagne or white wine at the last minute to warm, NEVER to boil.
Fill the empty pineapple shell with hot sauerkraut. Put the tasselled top on and serve immediately. Serves 6.

BOILED CHESTNUTS (CHESTNUT PURÉE)

1½ pounds chestnuts   *2 tablespoons butter*
2 cups boiling, salted   *¼ teaspoon pepper*
*   water*   *¼ cup hot cream*
2 stalks celery, chopped   *Dash of paprika*

Cover the chestnuts with cold water and bring to a boil. Boil for 30 minutes then drain and plunge the nuts into cold water. Loosen the shells with a paring knife and rub the skins off with a coarse towel.

Now cover the chestnuts with boiling, salted water, add the celery and cook until tender — about 25 minutes.

Drain the chestnuts, mash them with butter, pepper and cream. Whip as you would mashed potatoes. Heat through and serve, sprinkled with paprika. Serves 4.

PURÉE OF LENTILS

2 cups dried lentils	1 bay leaf
4 cups bouillon or stock	2 cloves
1 slice salt pork	2 tablespoons butter
2 sprigs parsley	¼ cup heavy
1 or 2 small onions,	cream
sliced	½ teaspoon salt
1 clove garlic	¼ teaspoon pepper

Wash the lentils and drain. Cover with water and soak all night. When ready to cook place the parsley, onions, garlic, bay leaf and cloves in a cheese cloth bag and put in the kettle with the lentils, bouillon and salt pork. Bring slowly to a boil, lower the heat and simmer until the lentils are tender — about 1½ hours.

Remove the herb bag after the first hour. If necessary add boiling water if the lentils are cooking too quickly.

When done put through a fine sieve or strainer. Set over heat and whip butter, cream and seasonings into the purée. Serves 4.

POTATOES PARISIENNE

8 large new potatoes   *2 tablespoons butter*
Boiling, salted water   *or bacon fat*
                    Salt and paprika

Wash and peel the potatoes. Cover with cold water and let stand for an hour. Drain. Cut into balls with a French cutter. Cover with boiling, salted water and cook until almost tender — 25 minutes. Drain.

Melt the butter or fat in a frying pan and fry the potato balls until light brown. Season with salt and paprika.

Now place them in a shallow pan in a hot oven (400 degrees) to crisp and brown. Add more butter or fat if needed. Serves 6.

DUMPLING BALLS

These are excellent with any stew.

2 cups sifted flour   *1 egg, beaten*
1 teaspoon salt   *3 tablespoons short-*
4 teaspoons baking   *ening, melted*
*   powder*   *Milk*
¼ teaspoon pepper   *4 to 6 cups bouillon*

Sift the dry ingredients together. Add the shortening and egg and beat smooth with a fork or wire whisk. Add enough milk to make a fairly moist dough. Form into 1 inch balls and drop into the boiling bouillon. Cover tightly and boil for 15 to 18 minutes, or until dumplings come to the surface.

Many cooks like to put croutons in the dumplings —
one in the center of each 1 inch ball. 6 servings.

HOMINY SOUFFLÉ

Particularly good with any game bird.

¾ cup hominy grits	3 egg yolks, beaten
1 cup boiling water	3 egg whites, beaten
2 cups milk	stiff
¼ cup melted butter	Salt

Pour hominy grits into the boiling water and cook, stirring constantly, for 2 minutes. Then put into a double
boiler over boiling water — but see that the bottom of
the upper part does not touch the water. Stir in 1 cup of
milk and cook for 30 minutes, stirring occasionally. Remove from the heat, add the second cup of milk, stir and
add the melted butter.

Replace over the boiling water and stir until smooth.

Beat the egg yolks well, remove pan from heat and stir
them in. Cool well, even overnight. (But NOT in the
refrigerator.)

45 minutes before serving fold the stiffly beaten egg
whites into the cold hominy. Preheat oven to 350 degrees. Put the mixture into a buttered baking dish and
bake for about 45 minutes. The soufflé should be golden
brown on top. Dot with butter. Serves 6.

If you wish add a cup of grated cheese to the cold mixture. I have done it often and like it very much.

TRUFFLES* — AN APPRECIATION

The ancients dedicated this black fungus to Venus believing that eating it encouraged love. In more modern times it has been said that those who wish to live virtuous lives should avoid truffles. Actually it is a wholesome, easily digested, delicately flavored food.

George Sand called it "The Fairy Apple." To Brillat-Savarin it was "the diamond of the kitchen." He considered it as important in grand cuisine as the ambergris is in making perfume, transforming sauces and other dishes into gastronomic works of art. It is worthy of these titles and of the accolades of epicures who appreciate fully the subtle flavor it imparts.

*Available in cans at the better grocers and specialty food shops.

GAME LEFTOVERS

In every kitchen there are leftovers — in the hunter's kitchen, particularly, because one never knows what or how much game will be brought home. To me game leftovers are exciting challenges and can result in dishes of exceptional appeal. Once you have had your fill of game, cooked as you like it, you'll enjoy the change-of-pace recipes like these offer.

In combination with bacon or ham, pork or veal, aromatic and piquant seasonings, cream or wine sauces, gravies and decorative garnishings, you can create little masterpieces that will be received happily by all who share them with you.

GAME SOUFFLÉ

Mince the leftovers (any kind of game) with a little onion then put through the meat grinder. Line a fireproof dish with mashed potatoes, then a layer of softly cooked sauerkraut (cooked 15 minutes). On this place a layer of game mixed with minced parsley, a little grated lemon peel and game seasoning. Another layer of sauerkraut goes on then a layer of game and finally, mashed potatoes. To top it off, cover with grated cheese and a little melted butter. Bake in a 375 degree oven until golden brown.

GAME OMELET

Mix sauted pieces of game with grated onion, minced parsley and caraway seeds and stir into an omelet mixture (beaten eggs with a little cold water). The amount of game will determine the size omelet. Pour into a well greased, heated omelet pan or skillet. When it is golden brown on one side, turn carefully and brown on the other.

Shake the pan occasionally to prevent sticking, and when finished to your satisfaction, slide onto a hot plate. Sprinkle with parsley and grated cheese and serve with a salad.

GAME HASH I

2 lbs. leftover game
(venison, duck,
moose, wild turkey,
hare)
2 tablespoons bacon fat
½ pint light cream

2 teaspoons capers
Salt and pepper
6 fried eggs
1 medium onion,
    minced

Cut the meat into very small squares. Fry the onion in the bacon fat until lightly browned. Add the meat, capers, salt, pepper and cream and simmer very slowly until it almost boils.

Serve with fried eggs on top — or bread croutons, if you prefer. 6 servings.

GAME HASH II

You can combine cooked game with raw pieces (side flaps
of venison, moose etc.). Boil in salted water together
with some carrots and/or turnips until tender. Put
through a meat grinder.
In a skillet, greased with butter or oil, brown lightly, a
finely minced onion. Add the meat and brown all over.
Mix in some flour or white sauce to thicken. Then, as you
prefer, pour in butter milk or sour cream; vinegar or
lemon juice; or a small glass of red wine. (Don't use
more than one of the above.) Season with soup seasoning and a good pinch of sugar. Serve with rice, noodles
or dumplings.

GAME MEAT LOAF

Grind whatever game you have — raw or cooked. If it is
very dry add some chopped bacon or lean or fat pork.
Season with minced onion and lemon peel, salt and pepper.

If you have 1 or 2 juniper berries add them. If not use a
teaspoon of gin. Mix with 1 or 2 beaten eggs and breadcrumbs (or white bread soaked in milk; be sure to press
out all the milk.) Make into loaf shape, place in a greased
loaf pan and bake in a 350 degree oven for about an hour.

Make a sauce with bouillon cubes and sour cream or buttermilk or red wine.

MEAT LOAF VARIATIONS

Filled Meat Loaf: Make meat loaf as above and fill with sliced, hard boiled eggs, dill pickles or strips of tender cooked tongue (preferably smoked tongue).

With Bacon Strips: Cover top with strips of bacon. Bake as above. Serve hot or cold.

With Mushrooms: Mix in lots of parsley and ½ pound of minced mushrooms. If they are very wet, fry them in a little fat for a few minutes and pour off the fat before adding them to the meat mixture.

With Cheese: Add ¼ to ½ pound of grated hard cheese and a bit more breadcrumbs.

GAME CROQUETTES

Grind game with a little fat pork, bacon or ham. Make a little brown sauce, add the game and heat through. Season with salt, pepper, minced onion, grated lemon peel, lemon juice, 1 or 2 crushed juniper berries (or a teaspoon of gin), a little sugar and soup seasoning. They should be strongly seasoned. Smooth into a greased pan and allow the mixture to cool.

Form long rolls, brush carefully with raw egg, roll in breadcrumbs and bake in a 350 degree oven until golden brown.

BIGON (POLISH HUNTER'S DISH)

Grind ½ pound of left overs, add a generous amount of minced parsley, 1 teaspoon anchovy paste, 1 or 2 small gherkins, chopped, 1 medium onion, minced and a pinch each of paprika and ginger.

Prepare a white sauce and mix the above with it. Add a little white wine and season with a little sugar and soup seasoning. Heat and serve with boiled or mashed potatoes.

GAMEBURGERS

Any game leftovers, cooked or raw, may be used. Put the meat through the grinder twice. From the amount of meat you will be able to determine the proportions of the other ingredients to arrive at the right flavor and consistency. (I'm *sure* you've made hamburgers before!)

The way I make them is with chopped bacon, minced onion, grated lemon peel, salt, pepper, 1 or 2 crushed juniper berries or a teaspoon of gin, 1 or 2 eggs and enough breadcrumbs to bind the mixture together. When thoroughly mixed (with your hands) make a round (3 or 4 inches diameter) loaf and cut off ¾ inch patties. Fry them or broil them. If broiled you might want to top them with cheese slices to make a delicious cheese gameburger.

GAMEBURGER PIQUANT

A nice variation from the above. Put the meat through the grinder twice. Then add 1 teaspoon of anchovy paste, plenty of minced parsley, celery leaves, chopped fine, salt, pepper, paprika, soup seasoning, 1 or 2 eggs and enough breadcrumbs to bind the other ingredients. Form patties as above and fry them in oil or other fat. Garnish each with crossed strips of crisp bacon and top with a slice of tomato.

SUNDAY NIGHT SUPPER

Use cooked leftovers and the same amount of bacon. Cut all into as even pieces as possible and place them in alternate layers with softly cooked sauerkraut in an oven proof dish. Make a mixture of 1 cup of light cream, 2 beaten eggs, a little salt and Bovril. Pour over and place in a 375 degree oven for 30 minutes or until brown. Serve with fried potatoes and salad and you have a Sunday night supper that will please everyone.

GAME SAUSAGE I

(ELISABETH, PRINCESS ALTENBURG)

10 lbs. venison or moose   *3 teaspoons sugar*
   meat   *1 tablespoon white*
4 lbs. fresh fat pork   *pepper*
7 tablespoons salt   *1 tablespoon saltpeter*

You may not have 10 pounds of meat available but you can adjust the other ingredients to the amount of game.

Raw venison or moose meat are required — neck and all other scrap meat may be used. But it must be without sinews and FRESH, in other words not hung. All blood must be wiped away.

First grind the game alone and for the second grinding add the fat pork. Then mix with all other ingredients and knead well for 10 minutes. Pack the mixture tightly into animal intestines or plastic bag, pushing it in hard so there is NO AIR IN THE BAGS (this is very important). Hang the bags in a cool room for 4 or 5 days so they really get dry. Then take them to your butcher — or a smoke house — and smoke for two weeks.

GAME SAUSAGE II

This sausage may be made out of all leftovers, no matter what game, using the lungs, heart, liver, etc. Remove all sinews from the raw game, add game liver (soaked in water for several hours or overnight, OR a piece of calves liver. For 2 parts game add one part bacon. Run all through the grinder twice.

Season the minced meat with salt, pepper, thyme, marjoram, grated lemon peel, pulverized juniper berries and a pinch of pimento or ground romano. Then make the mixture half fluid with hot water or, still better, white wine and put it into plastic bags as above.

Keep in a cool place or in the refrigerator. You may either fry or broil the sausage patties you form.

SOFT OR HARD ROLL PETITS PATÉS

Any game leftovers will do. Cut a soft or hard breakfast roll in half. Take out soft inside, butter it or spread with a little bacon fat. Fill with small pieces of game and leftover gravy. If there is not enough gravy add some sour cream, tomato sauce or consomme. Cover with a thick round piece of cheese, sprinkle with paprika and bake in 375 degree oven until the cheese has melted.

VENISON OR GAME PATÉ IN ASPIC

1 lb. raw venison   *of truffle pieces*
(shoulder)   *Salt and pepper*
½ lb. leftover game   *Thyme*
¼ lb. bacon   *Marjoram*
¼ lb. calf's liver   *2 egg yolks*
3 slices white bread   *1 tablespoon pistachios*
(crustless)   *1 tablespoon Madeira*
½ cup milk   *wine*
1 truffle or small tin

This is made in two stages: first, the cooked mixture, then the aspic.

Mix the raw and leftover meat with the white bread that has been soaked in milk and put it through the meat grinder. Next mix in the bacon, cut in cubes, calf's liver also cut in cubes, the sliced truffle and the Madeira. Add salt and pepper, ¼ teaspoon of marjoram, a pinch of thyme, pistachios and egg yolks and mix well.

Cover the inside of a Pyrex dish with sliced bacon. Fill with the mixture, cover with aluminum foil and a tight fitting lid. Place in a deep dish half filled with water and put into a 350 degree oven for 3 hours.

Turn out the mixture and let it stand until cold. Cut in ¼ inch slices. Then prepare the aspic of 1 can of consommé and 1 package (1 tablespoon) of gelatin.

GAME PATÉ

Use raw game (liver, heart, lungs — anything) as well as cooked leftovers: 1 pound more or less. Boil in salt water with bay leaf and onion rings. When tender, cool it and put it through the meat grinder twice. Mix with minced onion, 1 or 2 teaspoons of anchovy paste, salt, pepper, a little pimento, paprika, ginger, grated lemon peel and a small glass of cognac. Stir in 2 or 3 egg yolks and bind with bread crumbs.

Put the mixture into a greased form in a deep dish with water and roast in a 350 degree oven for 60 minutes. When cool turn the paté out onto a plate and serve it on toast with anchovies and sauce Remoulade (see page 199).

BAKED LEFTOVER GAME BREAD SLICES

Mince any kind of leftover game pieces. Mix with cranberries, grated lemon peel, salt, paprika and Bovril. Heap on buttered slices of white bread and bake in a 350 degree oven until golden brown.

These are wonderful served with vegetables or with a salad.

GAME SALAD

Cut any cooked leftover game into squares, strips or small slices allowing ¼ to ½ pound of meat per person. Add a few anchovy fillets, 1 tablespoon of capers, a few dill pickles, cut in cubes, and cubes of celery. (Cubed apple is good too.) Season with oil, vinegar, salt, pepper and a pinch of sugar. Use some thin mayonnaise if you so desire.

Put in the refrigerator so that the dressing has a chance to penetrate and, before serving, garnish with hard boiled egg slices, tomato slices, chopped parsley or chives.

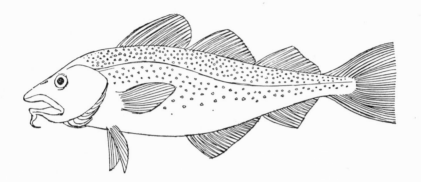

FISH LEFTOVERS

FISH OMELET

2 cups cold flaked fish
2 cups cold boiled pota-
    toes, diced
1 tablespoon minced
    onion

½ teaspoon salt
¼ teaspoon pepper
1 pinch tarragon
1 egg, beaten

Combine ingredients and fry in bacon fat until golden brown. Fold and serve like an omelet.

FISH CROQUETTES

2 cups leftover fish,
    flaked
Salt and pepper
Paprika

1 to 2 eggs beaten
Shredded lemon rind
½ onion, minced
Parlsey

Breadcrumbs

Mix all the ingredients together, binding the mixture with the breadcrumbs so that it holds together. Form into small croquettes and brown in fat until golden.

KEDGEREE

2 cups cold flaked fish   2 tablespoons minced
2 cups cooked rice (hot)   parsley
4 hard boiled eggs,   1 teaspoon salt
   chopped   ⅛ teaspoon pepper
½ cup light cream   ⅛ teaspoon curry

Add all the above to the hot rice and reheat for a few minutes in a double boiler. Sprinkle with chopped parsley and serve immediately.

FISH LOAF

Grind 1 pound of cold leftover fish. Add 1 finely minced onion, herbs, shredded lemon rind, a little lemon juice, salt, pepper, nutmeg, 3 or 4 tablespoons of breadcrumbs or 3 or 4 slices of white bread, soaked in milk and squeezed dry. Then put in a cup of cooked and shredded celery OR 3 tablespoons of thick tomato puree OR a few sprigs of marjoram depending on your taste. Form into a loaf, place in a well buttered form and bake in a 375 degree oven until brown.

INDEX